MARXISM AND PHILOSOPHY

MARXISM AND PHILOSOPHY

KARL KORSCH

Translated and introduced
by Fred Halliday

VERSO
London • New York

Published by Verso 2012

Published by New Left Books 1970

3 5 7 9 10 8 6 4

Verso
UK: 6 Meard Street, London W1F 0EG
US: 20 Jay Street, Suite 1010, Brooklyn, NY 11201
www.versobooks.com

Verso is the imprint of New Left Books

ISBN-13: 978-1-78168-027-8

British Library Cataloguing in Publication Data
A catalogue record for this book is available from the British Library

Library of Congress Cataloging-in-Publication Data
A catalog record for this book is available from the Library of Congress

Printed in the United States

Karl Korsch
An Introduction

Karl Korsch was born on 15 August 1886 in Todstedt, near Hamburg.[1] His father was a bank official who came originally from an East Prussian family of small farmers. After some time in Todstedt, the family moved to Meiningen, in Thuringia, where Korsch attended the local secondary school. Later he attended the universities of Munich, Berlin, Geneva and Jena. He studied law, economics and philosophy and was also a member of a 'Free Student Movement' which was opposed to the reactionary and nationalist student fraternities (*Verbindungen*) and aimed to establish contacts between the academic world and the socialist movement. In 1910 he acquired his doctorate at Jena, with a thesis on the onus of proof in admissions of guilt. It was published a year later in Berlin.

Between 1912 and 1914 Korsch continued his studies in London. He joined the Fabian Society, and was strongly influenced by the syndicalist movement. In his early years, he

1. The best sources for the biographical information on Korsch are Erich Gerlach's introduction and biographical notes to the 1966 edition of *Marxismus und Philosophie* (Europäische Verlagsanstalt, Frankfurt); Herman Weber's *Die Wandlung des deutschen Kommunismus* (Europäische Verlagsanstalt, 1969); and the special number of *Alternative* on Korsch (Berlin, April 1965, 41).

believed that these emphasized the positive content and actively democratic aspects of socialism, by contrast with the orthodox Marxism of the Second International which he thought defined itself merely negatively as the abolition of the capitalist mode of production. At the same time, he wrote articles for German periodicals on aspects of English life, including English law, the suffragettes, farm policy, Galsworthy and the state of English universities.[2] In 1913 he married Hedda Gagliardi, by whom he had two daughters. They remained together throughout his life and frequently cooperated in theoretical work.

On the outbreak of the First World War, in August 1914, Korsch returned to Germany. Because he opposed the war he was demoted from the rank of a reserve lieutenant to a corporal; but although he never carried a weapon, he was wounded and twice decorated with the Iron Cross. After the war, in 1919, he became a lecturer at Jena University.

The war marked the beginning of his active political life and of his most intense period of theoretical production. In 1917 he joined the Independent German Socialist Party (USPD) which had split from the official German Social Democratic Party (SPD) to the left. When the USPD itself split in 1920, Korsch went with the majority faction into the German Communist Party (the KPD) although he had reservations about the Twenty-one Points which formed the Leninist conditions for membership of the Communist International. In this period, after the November 1918 overthrow of the Kaiser and the declaration of the Weimar Republic, much of Europe, and particularly Germany, was in a state of revolu-

2. Cf. 'Die Fabian Society', *Die Tat*, IV, 8; 'Beiträge zur Kenntnis des englischen Rechts', *Zeitschrift für Internationales Recht*, XIV; 'Die Freiheit in England', *Die Tat*, V, 7; 'Probleme und Aussichten englischer Universitätsentwicklung', *Die Tat*, VI, 4; 'Galsworthy', *Die Tat*, V, 9.

tionary ferment. The Spartacist rising in Berlin (January 1919) and the Munich Soviet Republic (April 1919) were both bloodily suppressed. But for two years there was an active and widespread movement for workers' councils inspired by a varied set of Marxist and anarcho-syndicalist ideas.[3] Korsch participated actively in this movement which he believed to be realizing many of the ideas he had developed in pre-war London. He was a member of the Berlin Socialization Committee and contributed to the revolutionary magazine *Arbeiterrat*.

His writings on workers' councils over this period fall into two phases: between 1918 and 1920 they reflected the immediacy and optimism of the movement; between 1920 and 1922 they expressed its decline in activity and the need for more critical reflection. When the movement was at its height he concentrated on elaborating a hypothetical economic system for a national economy based on workers' councils. Each plant was to be run by a factory council, which was to be the constitutive institution of proletarian democracy. In *What is Socialization?* (March 1919) he sets out a system of economic organization, called 'industrial autonomy', in which every branch of the national industry would be run by a committee coordinating the interests of both producers and consumers.[4] Each individual factory would have a limited freedom within its industry. Decisions would relate to the volume of production, the conditions of work and the division of earnings. In the first stage of this system the means of production would be socialized and workers would still be paid according to output;

3. Cf. P. V. Oertzen, *Betriebsräte in der Novemberrevolution* (Droste Verlag, Düsseldorf, 1963).

4. His most important texts from this period are reprinted in *Schriften zur Sozialisierung* (Europäische Verlagsanstalt, 1969). His role and ideas are discussed in Oertzen, op. cit., and in G. E. Rusconi, 'Korsch e la strategia consiliare-sindicale', *Problemi del Socialismo*, no. 41, 1969.

in the second stage, labour itself would be socialized and workers would be paid according to their needs. In this work Korsch is concerned not only to provide the positive content he felt was absent from pre-war socialism, but also to attack the reformist and social-democratic concepts of 'nationalization' and 'workers' participation' then prevalent in Germany, which served to deflect the councils' movement from its revolutionary aims. These reformist conceptions found their expression in a Reichstag law of February 1920.

As German capitalism consolidated itself, and the councils' movement declined, Korsch tried to analyse the reasons for the failure of the upsurge of 1918–20. While other Marxists correctly stressed the absence of a revolutionary organization to seize power, Korsch emphasized that the theoretical and cultural preconditions for such a seizure of power were also lacking. 'In the fateful months after November 1918, when the organized political power of the bourgeoisie was smashed and outwardly there was nothing else in the way of the transition from capitalism to socialism, the great chance was never seized because the *socio-psychological* preconditions for its seizure were lacking. For there was nowhere to be found any decisive *belief* in the immediate realizability of a socialist economic system, which could have swept the masses along with it and provided a clear knowledge of the nature of the first steps to be taken.'[5] Korsch ascribed the defeat of the German November Revolution to the absence of ideological preparation and political leadership. This analysis characterized much of his subsequent work. His book *Arbeitsrecht für Betriebsräte* ('Labour Law for Factory Councils'), written in 1922, was based on a course of lectures he gave to workers, and represented an attempt to provide a proletarian law for workers'

5. *Schriften zur Sozialisierung*, p. 74.

councils.[6] Korsch's earlier juridical training is evident in this work, which argues that the law relating to labour is a crucial area of bourgeois ideology and expresses the productive relations constitutive of a capitalist society. Korsch thought it was a key ideological task of the revolutionary movement to prepare a proletarian legal expression of future socialist relations of production.[7] It may be said that this text on the councils, written after Korsch had joined the KPD, had a more Leninist character than his earlier work. In contrast to the Dutch leftists, Pannekoek and Gorter, it stresses the need for a party and for trade unions as well as for councils, although it still accords primacy to the councils within this triangular set of proletarian institutions.[8] It assumes throughout that the suspension of political life in the Soviets in Russia was a merely temporary occurrence, imposed on the Bolsheviks by famine and Civil War.

Korsch's work on factory councils and its incipient development towards Leninism contrasts with that of the Italian Marxist Antonio Gramsci, who was engaged in the Turin Soviet movement over the same period.[9] Like Korsch, Gramsci tried to theorize the spontaneous movement of workers' power released by the 1914–18 war. Both thought that a future revolutionary State could be prefigured by the

6. Reprinted, except for some sections on the 1920 Reichstag legislation, as *Arbeitsrecht für Betriebsräte* (Europäische Verlagsanstalt, 1968).

7. ibid., p. 26.

8. ibid., pp. 138ff.

9. Antonio Gramsci, 'Soviets in Italy', *New Left Review*, 51, with an introduction. Other relevant aspects of Gramsci's thought are discussed in John M. Cammett, *Antonio Gramsci and the Origins of Italian Communism* (Stanford University Press, 1967). This also narrates Gramsci's relations to Bordiga, Korsch's Italian ally in the inner-party struggles in the middle 1920s. It is because of this alliance that Korsch's group criticized Gramsci's work in *Ordine Nuovo* as 'an idealist infection of Italian Communism' (Gerlach, in *Schriften zur Sozialisierung*, p. 11).

direct establishment of nuclear proletarian institutions here and now. However, Korsch's elaborate hypothetical proletarian state in *What is Socialization?*, like Gramsci's early work, avoided the central problems of the revolutionary insurrection to overthrow the bourgeois State and the party organization necessary to accomplish it. After the defeat of the councils in 1920, both analysed the causes of this setback, but Gramsci went much further than Korsch in accepting the Leninist theory of the party as the indispensable organization of the proletariat to combat the bourgeois state. 'Revolution is like war,' Gramsci wrote, 'it must be minutely prepared by a working-class general staff.'[10] Korsch, on the other hand, went on to develop his theory of the subjective preconditions for revolution by a critique of orthodox Marxism for its failure to provide such a theory. There is however a certain parallel with Gramsci here too. Although Gramsci emphasized the importance of the party more than Korsch, he also stressed the need for struggle in the realm of civil society, in culture and ideology, since the power of the ruling class was protected by its ideological predominance, or hegemony, over all classes of capitalist society. A major task of the proletarian revolution, argue both Korsch and Gramsci, is struggle on the ideological front. For both of them positive intervention in the sphere of ideas had to start with a general critique of fatalistic and mechanist trends in the Marxism of the Second International.

Korsch expressed this emphasis on theory by writing works at two levels. On one level, he wrote a series of pedagogic brochures and articles, designed for party members, introducing and explaining the basic concepts of Marxism. Three of these appeared in 1922. *Kernpunkte der materialistischen*

10. *New Left Review*, 51, p. 27. For Korsch's own positive position on Lenin's theory of the party, and his opposition to that of Rosa Luxemburg, see 'Lenin und die Komintern' in *Die Internationale* 1924.

Geschichtsauffassung ('Elements of the Materialist Conception of History') began by setting out the basic relationship of theory to practice within the revolutionary movement, in an essay that anticipated many of the themes of *Marxism and Philosophy*. It then went on to illustrate various key Marxist concepts, like 'class struggle' and 'the dialectic', by a wide use of quotations, not only from Marx, Engels and Lenin, but also from the Gospels, Shakespeare, Hegel, Goethe and Schiller. Another similar work, *Quintessenz des Marxismus*, sets out basic principles of Marxism in the form of thirty-seven questions and answers. Finally, Korsch produced a popular edition of Marx's *Critique of the Gotha Programme* with a political introduction stressing the relevance of Marx's text to the immediate question then facing the workers' movement, the seizure of state power.[11]

On another level, Korsch now prepared an analysis of the historical degeneration of Marxist theory in the Second International and of the contemporary state of Marxism. This work was *Marxism and Philosophy*, published in 1923. It grew directly out of the interrelation of his own intellectual biography and the objective historical development of the German revolutionary movement. It starts by arguing that neither Marxists nor bourgeois philosophers had seen the historical connection between Hegel's dialectical idealism and Marx's dialectical materialism. They had also failed to understand why Hegelian philosophy died out in the 1840s. To do so would be to see the dialectical and material relationship between idealism and the bourgeoisie in its revolutionary phase, before 1848. Since Hegel's idealism expressed this heroic epoch of bourgeois development, it died out when the bourgeoisie ceased to be revolutionary. The new revolutionary class was the prole-

11. Korsch's Introduction is included in this volume, p. 145.

tariat, which found its theoretical expression in dialectical materialism. Hence the historical relationship between bourgeois philosophy and Marxist materialism could only be understood within the basic Marxist materialist outlook itself. Marxism is not a philosophy but the heir of philosophy.

The Second International had obscured this relationship because it had itself ceased to be revolutionary. It no longer embodied the principle that defined Marx's original work: the dialectical unity of a critical theory and a revolutionary practice. Instead theory had become merely a passive and static analysis of a given situation and no longer expressed any direct impulse towards revolution. Korsch tried to situate this crisis of theory within the history of Marxism and the European workers' movement as a whole. He thus made a novel and highly controversial attempt to apply Marx's materialist method to the history of Marxist theory itself. After 1917 a new revolutionary situation had emerged in Europe. Lenin re-established the unity of theory and practice, above all by his focus on the relationship between Marxism and the State. In what he conceived as an analogous enterprise, Korsch attempted to re-open the question of the relationship of Marxism to philosophy, and to ideology in general. Unlike the theorists of the Second International, Korsch acknowledged the specific autonomy of the ideological level within capitalist society and its practical consequence: bourgeois ideology will never disappear automatically, even after the revolution – it must be fought by the theory of scientific socialism. The mistake of vulgar Marxism was to fall into a 'transcendental underestimation' of the resilience of the intellectual and ideological apparatus of bourgeois society. Korsch's earlier work on proletarian law can be seen as a specific example of the kind of intellectual work he regarded as necessary in the struggle against this apparatus. On the other hand, mere academic criticism was futile. The material base of any society is in its socio-economic structure. This must be overthrown in practice if its intellectual superstructure is to be overcome in theory. 'One cannot abolish philosophy without realizing it.' It is only by grasping the historical relationship between the bourgeois revolution and its theoretical expression in idealist philosophy that the working class can overcome this philosophy and destroy bourgeois ideological power in practice.

Korsch's emphasis on the historical relationship of Marx to Hegel, and on the subjective preconditions for a successful revolution, parallel themes in George Lukács's *History and Class Consciousness*, which appeared as Korsch's work was going to press. In a laconic 'Afterword instead of a Foreword' Korsch wrote: 'So far as I have been able to establish, I am happily in fundamental agreement with the themes of the author (Lukács), which relate in many ways to the question raised in this work, if based on a broader philosophical foundation. In so far as there are still differences of opinion between us on particular issues of substance and method, I reserve a more comprehensive position for a later discussion.'[12] However, as he explains in his *Anti-Critique* of 1930, Korsch never did publish his view of Lukács's work, although he gradually came to see that there were more divergences between them than he at first realized. What most obviously came between them, and later prevented any fruitful cooperative development, was the political reaction of official Communism to their respective works, and their own divergent response to this. Condemned together, they responded in different ways. Lukács performed a partly tactical and partly sincere self-criticism and remained a member of the Communist movement. Korsch did not.

12. *Marxismus und Philosophie*, 1923, p. 71.

The immediate response of both Social Democrat and Communist spokesmen to *Marxism and Philosophy* was unequivocally hostile. In a defensive and self-justifying review that was an apology for his own renegacy, Kautsky in *Die Gesellschaft* avoided discussing any of Korsch's theses on Hegel and ideological struggle. He did, however, obliquely admit that Second International Marxism had ceased to be revolutionary: 'For Korsch, Marxism is nothing but a theory of social revolution. In reality, one of the most outstanding characteristics of Marxism is the conviction that social revolution is only possible under specific conditions, i.e. only in specific lands and periods. The Communist sect, to which Korsch belongs, has completely forgotten this.'[13]

The official Communist movement was equally hostile to *Marxism and Philosophy* and Zinoviev attacked Korsch, together with Lukács and Graziadei, in his opening speech at the Fifth World Congress of the Comintern in 1924, at which Korsch was a KPD delegate: 'Comrade Graziadei, in Italy, published a book containing a reprint of the articles he wrote, when he was a Social Democratic revisionist, attacking Marxism. This theoretical revisionism cannot be allowed to pass with impunity. Neither will we tolerate our Hungarian Comrade Lukács doing the same in the domain of philosophy and sociology.... We have a similar tendency in the German Party. Comrade Graziadei is a professor, Korsch is also a professor (*Interruptions:* "Lukács is also a professor!"). If we get a few more of these professors spinning out their theories, we shall be lost. We cannot tolerate such theoretical revisionism of this kind in our Communist International.'[14]

13. *Die Gesellschaft*, I, p. 310.
14. *Fifth Congress of the Communist International: Abridged Report* (published by the Communist Party of Great Britain), p. 17.

Korsch also came under heavy attack from leading Party philosophers, led by Abram Deborin and his pupil Luppol, in the Soviet Union – where *Marxism and Philosophy* was translated twice.[15] Deborin criticized both Korsch and Lukács for idealism although he himself was engaged in a fierce battle for the 'dialectical' against the 'mechanistic' school within Soviet philosophy; after apparently defeating the 'mechanists' in 1929 he was himself denounced for 'Menshevizing idealism' in 1931 by Stalin.

The importance attributed to *Marxism and Philosophy* within the Comintern, where it aroused a yet greater furore than Lukács's *History and Class Consciousness*, is partly to be explained by the fact that in the period immediately during and after its publication Korsch was one of the most prominent members of the KPD – then the major Communist Party in the world outside the USSR. In 1923 he was elected to the Thuringian Parliament and in October of that year he became Communist Minister of Justice in the Thuringian government. The Party was preparing for an armed insurrection and Korsch took the ministry on party instructions to facilitate the seizure of arms and the overthrow of the state apparatus when the revolution began. However the planned rising was cancelled, and when a local insurrection erupted in Hamburg it was successfully suppressed by the army.

The great defeat of October 1923 led to the banning of the KPD and the loss of fifty per cent of its membership. Within the Party the previous Brandler leadership was ousted and replaced by the 'left' leadership of Arkadi Maslow and Ruth

15. For Deborin's own writings (including his critical review of Lukács's *History and Class Consciousness*) see *Kontroversen über dialektischen und mechanistischen Materialismus*, Abram Deborin and Nikolai Bukharin (Suhrkamp Verlag, Frankfurt, 1969).

Fischer. The new line of the Party emphasized the need for more organized revolutionary preparation and rejected any united front policy towards the Social Democrats. In this move to the left, Korsch became one of the Party's leading spokesmen and editor of its theoretical journal, *Die Internationale.* He also became a Communist deputy to the Reichstag, a post he held until 1928.

The Weimar Republic KPD had within it a wide variety of political views, many of them to the left of the official position of the leadership.[16] These were only gradually eliminated and purged in the process of 'Bolshevization' which took place from 1924 to 1929, and that transformed the KPD into a party organized on strict Stalinist lines. Political debate centred on a number of issues – parliamentary and trade union tactics, developments in the Soviet Union and the Comintern, and the state of European capitalism. Although Korsch sided with the Fischer-Maslow group in opposition to Brandler after October 1923, he himself opposed their obedience to the Russian Party, and in particular the official view that capitalism had achieved a temporary stabilization and that a revolution was no longer immediately possible. As a delegate to the Fifth World Congress of the Comintern he was not only attacked for his views on philosophy by Zinoviev but was also assailed by Bukharin for printing an article in

16. The reorganization of the KPD over this period and the politics of the left opposition are discussed in: Ossip K. Flechtheim, *Die KPD in der Weimarer Republik* (Europäische Verlagsanstalt, 1969); Hermann Weber, *Die Wandlung des deutschen Kommunismus*, a detailed analysis of Bolshevization and the exclusion of the left from the KPD; and Siegfried Bahne, 'Zwischen "Luxemburgismus" und "Stalinismus": Die "ultralinke" Opposition in der KPD', *Vierteljahresheft für Zeitgeschichte*, vol. 9, 1961, pp. 359–83. The KPD position on Korsch can be found in 'Die bürgerliche Konterrevolution und der Renegat Korsch', *Die Internationale*, September 1926.

Die Internationale that was critical of Bukharin and the theory of the labour aristocracy: 'We must ask: how is it that the editor of *Die Internationale* cannot exercise censorship? (Korsch: It was merely brought up for discussion). Comrades, we cannot bring up every bit of piffle for discussion. That is too much.'[17] The Comintern Congress revealed Korsch's growing break with the Fischer-Maslow group. The latter allied with the Russian leadership, while Korsch formed an opposition bloc with the Italian left faction led by Amadeo Bordiga. In February 1925 he was dismissed from the editorship of *Die Internationale* and from then onwards was in declared opposition to the Party leadership.

The Tenth Congress of the KPD in July 1925 voted for the organizational 'Bolshevization' of the Party. This meant both tighter centralist control and a more unswerving support for official Soviet positions. It was followed soon afterwards by the ousting of the Fischer-Maslow leadership, a consequence of the downfall of its patron Zinoviev in Russia, and its replacement by Thälmann and his associates. The KPD now reiterated that there had been a 'relative stabilization' in world capitalism and that the major political danger was a 'monarchist' one, represented by Hindenburg. Korsch's group opposed this analysis, and constituted itself in March 1926 around the magazine *Kommunistische Politik*. Known as the 'Entschiedene Linke' – 'Resolute Lefts' – they were at first a faction within the KPD. Their platform [18] began by

17. *Fifth Congress of the Communist International*, p. 135.

18. Summarized in Bahne, op. cit., pp. 372ff. and reprinted in Karl Korsch, *Der Weg der Komintern* (Berlin, 1926). Korsch's political articles over this period include 'Der Kampf der Linken um die Komintern', *Kommunistische Politik*, 18, 1926, and 'Zehn Jahre Klassenkämpfe in Sowjetrussland', ibid., 17–18, 1927.

stating that capitalism had not been stabilized and there existed 'all the objective requirements for concrete revolutionary politics'. The KPD should abandon its 'parliamentary cretinism' for a 'clear revolutionary class politics' and forge a socialist state built on workers' councils. The organization and mobilization of the unemployed and the creation of breakaway trade unions was a political priority in Germany. Any United Front with the SPD was rejected.

These latter ultra-left positions were reflected in the international outlook of the Korsch-Katz group. They were opposed to the New Economic Policy and Katz's group judged that the Soviet State was now a 'dictatorship of the Kulaks' and referred to Stalin as a *Bauernnapoleon*. Korsch argued that the Comintern had become an instrument of Russian foreign policy, and that the theory of 'stabilization' reflected the needs of a defensive state trying to form an alliance with world capitalism. Korsch supported the Russian 'workers' opposition' led by Shlyapnikov and Sapronov, but opposed the Left Opposition led by Trotsky. Trotsky for his part firmly condemned Korsch's wild judgements of the USSR, and the Left Opposition was officially to dissociate itself from his positions in its famous platform of 1927.[19]

The Korsch-Katz faction at first tried to fight within the KPD and the Comintern, but at the sixth Plenum of the Enlarged Executive Committee of the Communist International, in February-March 1926, orders were given for a more thorough purge of the German Party. Korsch was attacked by Bukharin for his analysis of the Comintern. Denounced by Zinoviev as 'an insane petty bourgeois', Korsch was given an ultimatum to relinquish his Reichstag seat or face expul-

19. For Trotsky's view of Korsch, see 'La Défense de l'URSS et l'Opposition', *Écrits*, vol. 1, Paris, 1955.

sion from the KPD. He refused to comply with this and was expelled in April 1926. He remained politically active for two years and kept his place in the Reichstag (in 1927 he was the only deputy to oppose the Soviet-German Trade Agreement). However, the ultra-left were driven out of the KPD and soon fell apart into many small groups. In April 1926 Korsch broke with the group around Katz in Hanover. The latter had split the local branch of the Communist youth organization and used its followers to occupy the offices of the KPD paper there. Korsch criticized this as a provocation to the Party leadership; he also wanted to try to work with the deposed leadership of Fischer and Maslow, which Katz rejected. Katz for his part attacked Korsch for trying to be 'another Lenin'. In September 1926 the 'Entschiedene Linke' group split, and Korsch's followers consolidated around the journal *Kommunistische Politik* which he subsidized from his Reichstag salary. At its Third Congress in May 1927 the *Kommunistische Politik* decided to adopt a status intermediate between that of the KPD faction and a new Party, but opposition throughout the communist movement was now in retreat. Korsch had international contacts with Norwegian left communists and with the Italian group around Bordiga; but in 1928 *Kommunistische Politik* ceased to appear and Korsch's period as a member of a political organization was over.

After 1928 Korsch continued to write and to lecture, and began a close intellectual friendship with Bertolt Brecht who had first started to attend Korsch's lectures on Marxism two years earlier. In February 1933, on the night of the Reichstag fire, Korsch gave his last political talk and had to flee from Germany the same night. The period 1928–33 had been one of considerable intellectual production. In 1929 he wrote a long attack on Kautsky, *Die materialistische Geschichtsauffassung*, and in 1930 reissued *Marxism and Philosophy* prefaced by an

Anti-Critique defending and elaborating his positions of 1923. In his 1931 *Theses on Hegel and the Revolution*[20] Korsch subsequently argued that Hegel's philosophy was the culmination of the ideology of the Enlightenment which expressed the fulfilment and the limits of bourgeois thought. It was thus both a philosophy of revolution and of restoration. This ambiguous dialectic was taken over by Marx and Engels, and Lenin, and their materialism was hence transitional: 'What was thereby created is a theory of proletarian revolution, not as it developed out of its own foundation, but on the contrary, as it emerged from the bourgeois revolution; given this relation, its form and content still bear the marks of Jacobinism as the theory of the bourgeois revolution.'

In exile Korsch continued his theoretical work and in 1938 he published *Karl Marx* – an analysis of Marx's mature theory rather than a biography.[21] *Marxism and Philosophy* studies the emergence of Marxism from classical bourgeois philosophy; *Karl Marx* shows how it simultaneously emerged from classical economic theory. Ricardo, like Hegel, took bourgeois thought to its limits and in doing so revealed the inner contradictions of it as a class ideology. Korsch traces the gradual development of Marx's thought from philosophy to science, through the initial passages in which the economy is given primacy in the Introduction to the *Critique of Hegel's Philosophy of Right*, to 'its first scientific expression, in his 1847 lectures to the German Workers Association in Brussels'.[22] *Karl Marx* expounds a central theme that is present, if in an understated fashion, in the original *Marxism and Philosophy*.

20. Reprinted in *alternative*, 41.

21. *Karl Marx* (Chapman and Hall, London, 1938; reprinted in New York, 1963).

22. Chapter 4, 'Scientific versus Philosophical Criticisms of Political Economy.' This is a more elaborate version of his account in *Marxism and Philosophy*, note 66, p. 85 below.

Korsch argues that the early Marx was still under the influence of philosophical residues, and only in his later work, constituted by a critique of political economy, did Marxism become a genuine science. Korsch adds that Marx never completely freed himself of his earlier philosophical formation, even in his later writings.[23]

Korsch's work has often been assimilated to that of Lukács and other intellectuals who re-emphasized Hegel's influence on Marx and the central importance of concepts such as 'alienation' in Marx's thought. *Karl Marx*, however, explicitly contrasts the 'pre-scientific' philosophical analysis of alienated labour in the early writings to the later scientific analysis of commodity fetishism in *Capital.* Korsch always stressed the superiority of Marx's later works, while equally insisting that Marx's economic theory was not a merely analytical system, but a *revolutionary critique* of the capitalist social order. This theme runs through his work, from his 1922 introduction to the *Critique of the Gotha Programme* to his 1938 book on Marx. Korsch's concern with philosophy was not an attempt to show Marx to be 'philosophical' or to derive sustenance from the 'early Marx'. Its aim was to show that Marx transcended 'philosophy' and yet inherited the dialectical interrelation of theory and practice that characterized classical idealism, giving it for the first time a materialist foundation. *Karl Marx* reiterates that 'Marx's materialistic science, being a strictly empirical investigation into definite historical forms of society, does not need a philosophical support'.[24]

Korsch's exile was marked by a deepening of his relationship with Brecht.[25] Brecht later said that he chose Korsch and

23. *Karl Marx*, p. 231.

24. ibid., p. 169.

25. Cf. the special issue of *alternative*, 41, on Korsch and Bertolt Brecht. This includes Korsch's annotations on Brecht's draft of the

the sociologist Fritz Sternberg as his Marxist instructors because they were not orthodox Party thinkers. In spite of their political differences, Korsch and Brecht kept up their relationship till Brecht's death in 1956. After 1933 Korsch and Brecht lived in Denmark and worked together, and when Korsch emigrated to the USA in 1936 they corresponded with each other. Korsch's *Karl Marx* inspired Brecht to try to rewrite the *Communist Manifesto* in hexameters, along the lines of Lucretius's *De rerum natura*, and in 1945 Brecht sent his draft to Korsch for comment. His letter concludes: 'Ich hoffe, Sie stöhnen nicht zu sehr, aber Sie wissen, lehrer sind Sie lebenslänglich, so take it easy. herzlich Ihr alter b'[26]. How deeply Korsch influenced Brecht is unclear, and it is speculative to argue that Brecht was influenced by Korsch's theory of ideological struggle in developing his own conception of drama. It is similarly uncertain whether differences between Korsch and Lukács immanent in their theoretical works are expressed more clearly in the conflicting aesthetic theories of Lukács and Brecht. Brecht and Korsch disagreed politically, but Brecht once wrote to Korsch that 'we have long disagreed in our evaluation of the USSR, but I almost believe that your position on the USSR is not the only one which can be derived from your scientific discoveries'.[27] When Korsch appears in Brecht's *Me Ti: Buch der Wendungen*, thinly disguised as Ko and Ka-osh, the main topic of discussion between the two is Stalinism.

---

versified *Manifesto*, a selection from Korsch's writings, and an article by W. Rasch on Korsch, 'Brechts marxistischer Lehrer'.

26. *alternative*, 41, p. 45. 'I hope you are not moaning too much, but you know that you are my teacher for life, so take it easy, affectionately your old b.'

27. *alternative*, 41, p. 99.

From 1936 to his death in 1961 Korsch lived in the USA. He taught sociology at Tulane University in New Orleans between 1943 and 1945, and from 1945 until 1950 he worked with the International Institute of Social Research, New York. At the same time he published a number of articles on Marxist theory.[28] He also carried out research on field theory with Kurt Lewin, traces of which can already be found in his emphasis on quantification and empirical findings in *Karl Marx*.[29]

By the early fifties, however, Korsch was evidently afflicted by the isolation of his position and by an increasing pessimism. In exile, cut off from any direct relationship to political struggle, and writing at the height of the Cold War, he fell into despair, reneging any connection with Marxism.[30] However, after 1953 his hopes for change in the Soviet Union revived, and his later years were marked by an increasing interest in the colonial world. Before the victory of the Chinese Revolution, he wrote an introduction to a planned volume of Mao Tse-Tung's essays, stressing their theoretical originality, and he had an optimistic perspective on developments in Asia and Africa.[31]

28. 'Why I am a Marxist', *Modern Monthly*, IX, 2, and other articles in *Council Correspondence, Modern Quarterly, Living Marxism* and *Partisan Review*.

29. *Karl Marx*, p. 236. Cf. Karl Korsch and Kurt Lewin, 'Mathematical Constructs in Psychology and Sociology', *Journal of Unified Sciences*, vol. 9, 1939.

30. See the annex to the French edition of *Marxism and Philosophy*, pp. 185–7.

31. Mao Tse-tung's emphasis on revolutionary ideas as concrete forces has some analogies with Korsch's theses on ideological struggle. On Korsch's interest in the colonial world see also 'Independence comes to the Philippines', *Asia*, XXI, 11, 1947.

In 1956 he made a last trip to Europe and in the same year there began his long, fatal illness. He died in Belmont, Massachusetts, on 21 October 1961. His wife, Dr Hedda Korsch, survives him.

Korsch was one of the most interesting and original, if erratic, Marxist theorists in the West during the twenties and thirties.[32] Among his contemporaries, he had an exceptional knowledge and understanding not only of the writings of Marx and Engels themselves, but also of the classical bourgeois thinkers who preceded them. The key to his fate is provided by his own constant emphasis on the unity of theory and practice, for he himself, and his work, were victims of the Stalinization of the European workers' movement after Lenin's death. Refusing to accept the bureaucratized political leadership of the KPD, he lapsed into ultra-leftism and became cut off from the working class; in exile, he ended by abandoning Marxism. His personal trajectory was only one of the many fatal consequences of the defeat of the socialist revolution in Western Europe after the First World War. But it is the re-emergence of revolutionary class politics in the advanced capitalist society of the West today that has revived interest in his work and provides an opportunity for Marxists critically to reassess it.

Fred Halliday
July 1970

32. The most competent and comprehensive recent discussion of Korsch's ideas are to be found in G. E. Rusconi, *La Teoria Critica* (Il Mulino, Bologna, 1968) and Giuseppe Vacca, *Lukács o Korsch?* (De Donato, Bari, 1969). Both discuss Korsch's relation to Lukács, and *Karl Marx* as well as *Marxism and Philosophy*.

A Note on this Edition

This English edition of Korsch's *Marxism and Philosophy* and his *Anti-Critique* is a translation of the German text of the 1966 Europäische Verlagsanstalt reprint of the 1930 edition. It does not include three other minor texts on dialectical materialism from the period 1922–24 that Korsch included in his 1930 edition, which are mainly restatements of theses already contained in *Marxism and Philosophy*. In their place I have added two important early texts which exemplify the methodological approach to Marx's work recommended by *Marxism and Philosophy* – study of the concrete historical relationship between Marx's theory and practice. The first, on Marx's *Critique of the Gotha Programme*, served as an introduction to a 1922 edition of the *Critique*; the second, 'The Marxism of the First International', was published in *Die Internationale* in 1924.

Translation of Korsch poses a number of problems. These are partly due to the difficulties generally associated with the translation of Hegelian terminology into English. They are also partly due to the highly involved and labyrinthine prose which Korsch adopted in *Marxism and Philosophy*, which becomes at times a torrent of parentheses, qualifications, repetitions and reformulations. The aim of this translation has been to provide a clear and readable English version of the German; sentences have frequently been broken up and restructured to make them more accessible.

The Hegelian term *Aufhebung* has been variously translated as 'supersession', 'transcendence' and 'abolition' where each of these words was most apposite. *Geist* and *geistig* have usually been rendered as 'mind' and 'mental', 'intellect' and 'intellectual', since the English words 'spirit' and 'spiritual' have stronger religious connotations than the German. *Wissenschaft* has sometimes been rendered as 'science' and sometimes as 'knowledge'.

Where possible I have given English sources for quotations that Korsch uses, but have sometimes varied the available translations. The English editions of Marx, Engels and Lenin used are as follows: Marx and Engels, *Selected Works* (Moscow, 1962), 2 vols. (volume I contains the *Communist Manifesto*, *The Eighteenth Brumaire of Louis Bonaparte*, the *Preface to the Critique of Political Economy*, and the *Inaugural Address to the Working Men's International Association*; and volume II contains the *Critique of the Gotha Programme*, *Socialism: Utopian and Scientific*, and *Ludwig Feuerbach and the End of Classical German Philosophy*); Marx and Engels *On Religion* (Moscow, n.d.), which contains the *Introduction to the Critique of Hegel's Philosophy of Right*, and the *Theses On Feuerbach*; *The German Ideology* (Lawrence and Wishart, London, 1965); *A Contribution to the Critique of Political Economy* (Chicago, 1904), although the Preface is more easily available in the *Selected Works* and the references are to this latter work; *Anti-Dühring* (Moscow, 1959); *Capital*, Volume I (Moscow, 1961). The edition of Lenin referred to is the Moscow English edition of the *Collected Works*.

F.H.

Marxism and Philosophy [1923]

We must organize a systematic study of the Hegelian dialectic from a materialist standpoint.
Lenin, 1922
'On the Significance of Militant Materialism'

Until very recently, neither bourgeois nor Marxist thinkers had much appreciation of the fact that the relation between Marxism and philosophy might pose a very important theoretical and practical problem. For professors of philosophy, Marxism was at best a rather minor sub-section within the history of nineteenth-century philosophy, dismissed as 'The Decay of Hegelianism'.[1] But 'Marxists' as well tended not to

1. Thus Kuno Fischer in his nine-volume *Geschichte der neueren Philosophie* devotes only one page (p. 1170) of the double volume concerned with Hegelian philosophy to (Bismarckian) 'State Socialism' and to 'Communism'. Their respective founders he names as Ferdinand Lassalle and Karl Marx: the latter is dispatched in two lines. He only quotes Friedrich Engels in order indirectly to cast a little discredit on his professional colleagues. In Überweg's *Grundriss der Geschichte der Philosophie vom Beginn des XIX. Jahrhunderts bis auf die Gegenwart*

lay great stress on the 'philosophical side' of their theory, although for quite different reasons. Marx and Engels, it is true, often indicated with great pride that historically the German workers' movement had inherited the legacy of classical German philosophy in 'scientific socialism'.[2] But they did not mean by this that scientific socialism or communism were primarily 'philosophies'.[3] They rather saw the task of their 'scientific socialism' as that of definitively overcoming and

(11th edition, Austria, 1916) there are *two* pages (pp. 208–9) devoted to the life and teachings of Marx and Engels; and there is also a mention of the materialist conception of history which in the space of a few lines is stated to be of importance for the history of philosophy, and is defined as 'the exact inversion of Hegel's idealist conception'. F. A. Lange in his *Geschichte des Materialismus* only mentions Marx in some historical footnotes where he is described as the 'greatest living expert on the *history of political economy*'; he takes no notice of Marx and Engels as theoreticians. This attitude is typical even of authors who devote monographs to the 'philosophical' content of Marxism. Cf. Benno Erdmann, 'The Philosophical Premisses of the Materialist Conception of History', *Jahrbuch für Gesetzgebung, Verwaltung und Volkswirtschaft*, XXXI (1916), pp. 919ff, especially pp. 970–2. Further examples are given later.

2. This is literally stated in the famous closing sentence of Engels's *Ludwig Feuerbach and the End of Classical German Philosophy*. Similar formulations are found in almost all the works of Marx and Engels, from the most varied periods of their lives, e.g. in the final sentence of the preface to the first edition of Engels's *Socialism: Utopian and Scientific*.

3. Cf. especially the polemics in the *Communist Manifesto* of 1847–8 against German or 'true' socialism, and the introductory statements of an article on German socialism which Engels published in *Almanach du Parti Ouvrier pour 1892*. Engels, apparently in complete agreement with the bourgeois philosophy of history, describes pre-1848 German socialism, which was 'dominated from the start by the name of Marx', as 'a theoretical movement that arose from the ruins of Hegel's philosophy'. He calls the followers of this trend 'ex-philosophers' and straightforwardly contrasts them to the 'workers' who according to him made up the other of the two trends which fused in 1848 to form German communism.

superseding the form and content, not only of all previous bourgeois idealist philosophy, but thereby of philosophy altogether. Later I shall have to explain in more detail what, according to the original conception of Marx and Engels, the nature of this supersession was or was intended to be. For the moment I merely record that historically this issue simply ceased to be a problem as far as most later Marxists were concerned. The manner in which they dealt with the question of philosophy can best be described in the vivid terms in which Engels once described Feuerbach's attitude to Hegelian philosophy: Feuerbach simply 'shoved' it 'unceremoniously aside'.[4] In fact, very many later Marxists, apparently in highly orthodox compliance with the masters' instructions, dealt in exactly the same unceremonious way not only with Hegelian philosophy but with philosophy as a whole. Thus, for example, Franz Mehring more than once laconically described his own orthodox Marxist position on the question of philosophy by saying that he accepted 'the rejection of all philosophic fantasies' which was 'the precondition for the masters' (Marx and Engels) immortal accomplishments'.[5] This statement came from a man who could with justice say that he had 'concerned himself with the philosophical origins of Marx and Engels more thoroughly

4. *Ludwig Feuerbach*, in Marx and Engels, *Selected Works*, vol. II, p. 368.

5. *Neue Zeit*, 28, I, p. 686. There are similar statements in the chapter on *The German Ideology* in Mehring's biography of Marx, *Karl Marx* (London, 1936), pp. 109ff. One can see how little Mehring has understood the meaning of these works of Marx and Engels (which unfortunately have still not been published in full), by comparing his statements with the corresponding sections of Gustav Mayer's biography of Engels, *Friedrich Engels* (1920), pp. 234–61. (*Translator's Note:* The 1936 English edition of Mayer's biography is a shortened and rewritten version of the German original, and does not contain the passages mentioned by Korsch.)

than anyone else', and it is extremely significant for the generally dominant position on all philosophical problems found among the Marxist theoreticians of the Second International (1889–1914). The prominent Marxist theoreticians of the period regarded concern with questions that were not even essentially philosophical in the narrower sense, but were only related to the general epistemological and methodological bases of Marxist theory, as at most an utter waste of time and effort. Of course, whether they liked it or not, they allowed discussion of such philosophical issues within the Marxist camp and in some circumstances they took part themselves. But when doing so they made it quite clear that the elucidation of such problems was totally irrelevant to the practice of proletarian class struggle, and would always have to remain so.[6] Such a conception was, however, only self-evident and logically justified given the premiss that Marxism as a theory and practice was in essence totally unalterable and involved no specific position on any philosophical questions whatever.

6. An interesting instance of this is a small clash whose traces can be found in *Neue Zeit* 26, I, pp. 695, 898. The editor (Karl Kautsky) had printed an introductory comment on an article he was publishing by Bogdanov on 'Ernst Mach and the Revolution'. In this comment the anonymous translator felt himself bound to censure Russian Social Democracy because the 'extremely serious *tactical* differences' between Bolsheviks and Mensheviks were 'exacerbated' by 'what we consider to be the *quite independent* question of whether Marxism is epistemologically in agreement with Spinoza and Holbach or with Mach and Avenarius'. The editorial board of the Russian Bolshevik *Proletary* (i.e. Lenin) was compelled to reply to this and to state that 'this philosophical conflict is in fact not an issue of inner party dispute and, in the opinion of the editors, it should not become so' ('Statement of the Editors of *Proletary*', Lenin, *Collected Works*, vol. 13, p. 447). It is however well known that the man who wrote this formal disclaimer, the great tactician Lenin, later in the same year published his philosophical work *Materialism and Empirio-Criticism*.

This meant that it was not regarded as impossible, for example, for a leading Marxist theoretician to be a follower of Arthur Schopenhauer in his private philosophical life.

During that period, therefore, however great the contradictions between Marxist and bourgeois theory were in all other respects, on this one point there was an apparent agreement between the two extremes. Bourgeois professors of philosophy reassured each other that Marxism had no philosophical content of its own – and thought they were saying something important *against* it. Orthodox Marxists also reassured each other that their Marxism by its very nature had nothing to do with philosophy – and thought they were saying something important *in favour* of it. There was yet a third trend that started from the same basic position; and throughout this period it was the only one to concern itself somewhat more thoroughly with the philosophical side of socialism. It consisted of those 'philosophizing socialists' of various kinds who saw their task as that of 'supplementing' the Marxist system with ideas from *Kulturphilosophie* or with notions from Kant, Dietzgen or Mach, or other philosophies. Yet precisely because they thought that the Marxist system needed philosophical supplements, they made it quite clear that in their eyes too Marxism in itself lacked philosophical content.'[7]

7. They attributed this to a weakness in Marxist theory and not, as the 'orthodox Marxists' did, to an advance registered by socialism in developing from a philosophy to a science; but this meant that they tried to rescue all or part of the remaining content of socialist theory. From the very start they were on the side of their bourgeois opponents in the battle between bourgeois and proletarian science. They merely tried to avoid the inevitable conclusion as long as was possible. But the events of crisis and war after 1914 made it impossible to continue to avoid the question of proletarian revolution, and the real character of *all kinds* of philosophizing socialism became as clear as could ever be

Nowadays it is rather easy to show that this purely *negative* conception of the relation between Marxism and philosophy, which we have shown to be held in apparent unanimity by bourgeois scholars as well as by orthodox Marxists, arose in both cases from a very superficial and incomplete analysis of historical and logical development. However, the conditions under which they both came to this conclusion *in part* diverge greatly, and so I want to describe them separately. It will then be clear that in spite of the great difference between the motives on either side, the two sets of causes do coincide in *one* crucial place. Among *bourgeois scholars* in the second half

---

desired. It was not only such overtly anti-Marxist and un-Marxist philosophizing socialists as Bernstein and Koigen, but also most of the philosophizing Marxists (Kantian, Dietzgenian and Machian Marxists) who since then have shown, in word and deed, that they have not really passed the standpoint of bourgeois society. This applies not only to their philosophy, but by necessary extension also to their political theory and practice. There is no need to provide examples of the bourgeois-reformist character of Kantian Marxism, as it can hardly be doubted. As for the path along which Machian Marxism is bound to lead its followers (and has lead most of them already), this was clearly shown by Lenin in his 1908 dispute with empirio-criticism. Dietzgenian Marxism has already gone part of the way along the same road, and this is shown by a little pamphlet written by Dietzgen's son (1923). This rather naïve 'neo-Marxist' does not just congratulate his 'guarantor' Kautsky for having abandoned most 'antique Marxist' positions, he also expresses his regret that Kautsky, having relearnt so much, should still retain some traces of them (p. 2). But David Koigen is the best example of how sound Mehring's political instinct was when he rejected philosophy altogether in the face of philosophical fantasies *like these*. To realize this one need only read the highly considerate criticism Mehring made of Koigen's completely immature early philosophical writings ('Neo-Marxism', *Neue Zeit*, 20, I, pp. 385ff., and Marx-Engels, *Nachlass* II, p. 348), and then realize how rapidly this philosopher, under Bernstein's patronage in 1903, developed into the most superficial 'cultural socialist' and anti-Marxist, and finally ended up as one of the most confused and reactionary romantics. (On this last phase see, for example, Koigen's article in *Zeitschrift für Politik*, 1922, pp. 304ff.)

of the nineteenth century there was a total disregard of Hegel's philosophy, which coincided with a complete incomprehension of the relation of philosophy to reality, and of theory to practice, which constituted the living principle of all philosophy and science in Hegel's time. On the other hand *Marxists* simultaneously tended in exactly the same way increasingly to forget the original meaning of the dialectical principle. Yet it was this that the two young Hegelians Marx and Engels, when they were turning away from Hegel in the 1840s, had quite deliberately rescued from German idealist philosophy and transferred to the materialist conception of history and society.[8]

First I shall summarize the reasons why, since the middle of the nineteenth century, *bourgeois* philosophers and historians have progressively abandoned the dialectical conception of the history of philosophy; and why they have therefore been incapable of adequately analysing and presenting the independent essence of Marxist philosophy and its significance within the general development of nineteenth-century philosophy.

One could perhaps argue that there were much more immediate reasons for the disregard and misinterpretation of Marxist philosophy, and that there is therefore absolutely no need for us to explain its suppression by reference to the abandonment of the dialectic. It is true that in nineteenth-century writing on the history of philosophy, a conscious class instinct undeniably contributed to the perfunctory treatment of Marxism, and, what is more, to a similar treatment of such bourgeois 'atheists' and 'materialists' as David Friedrich

8. Engels, *Anti-Dühring* (Moscow, 1959), p. 16 (preface to the second edition of 1885). Cf. similar statements by Marx at the end of his postscript to the second edition of *Capital*, 1873.

Strauss, Bruno Bauer and Ludwig Feuerbach. But we would only have a very crude idea of what in reality constitutes a very complex situation if we simply accused bourgeois philosophers of having consciously subordinated their philosophy, or history of philosophy, to class interest. There are of course instances which do correspond to this crude thesis.[9] But in general the relation of the philosophical representatives of a class to the class which they represent is a good deal more complex. In his *Eighteenth Brumaire* Marx deals specifically with interconnections of this kind. He says there that the class as a whole creates and forms 'an entire superstructure of distinct and peculiarly formed sentiments, illusions, modes of thought and views of life' out of its 'material foundations'. A part of the superstructure that is 'determined by class' in this way, yet is particularly remote from its 'material and economic foundation', is the philosophy of the class in question. This is most obvious as regards its content; but it also applies

9. The best examples of this are the following statements by E. von Sydow in his *Der Gedanke des Idealreichs in der idealistischen Philosophie von Kant bis Hegel* (1914), pp. 2–3: 'In so far as the idea of the Ideal is historicized, it loses its explosive force, for it is the Ideal which, in German idealism, renders history logical and transforms it from a "chain of events" into a "series of concepts". If the Ideal is a logico-historical necessity, then it is premature and pointless to strive for it. This elucidation of the concept of the Ideal was the achievement of the absolute Idealists. It is they whom we must thank if the social and economic order we have today prevails into the foreseeable future. While the ruling classes freed themselves from the historical phantasmagoria of idealism and often converted their will to action into the courage to act, the proletariat still believes in the materialist débris derived from the idealist system. It is to be hoped that this felicitous situation will continue for a long time. It was Fichte who contributed most to this achievement, as in all other questions of principle.' Von Sydow remarks quite explicitly in a footnote that this fact 'could be invoked against those who claim more or less openly that *philosophy is politically unimportant*'.

in the last instance to its formal aspects.[10] If we want to understand the complete incomprehension of the philosophical content of Marxism on the part of bourgeois historians of philosophy, and really to understand it in Marx's sense of the word – that is 'materialistically and therefore scientifically'[11] – we must not be content to explain this phenomenon directly and immediately by its 'earthly kernel' (namely class consciousness and the economic interests which it conceals 'in the last instance'). Our task is to show in detail the *mediations* of the process whereby even those bourgeois philosophers and historians who sincerely try to investigate 'pure' truth with the greatest 'objectivity' are bound completely to overlook the the philosophical content of Marxism or are only able to interpret it in an inadequate and superficial way. For our purposes the most important of these mediations is undoubtedly the fact that since the middle of the nineteenth century the whole of bourgeois philosophy, and especially, the bourgeois writing of the history of philosophy, has for socio-economic reasons abandoned Hegelian philosophy and the dialectical method. It has returned to a method of philosophy, and of writing the history of philosophy, which renders it

10. Cf. on this Marx, *The Eighteenth Brumaire of Louis Bonaparte* (Marx and Engels, *Selected Works*, vol. I) especially pp. 272, 275 (on the relationship of the ideological representatives of a class to the class as a whole which they represent); and Engels, *Ludwig Feuerbach* (*Selected Works*, vol. II), p. 397 – on philosophy. In this context one could also quote the remark in Marx's doctoral thesis which is a general critique of attempts to explain a philosopher's mistakes by 'questioning his individual consciousness' instead of objectively 'reconstructing his essential forms of consciousness, erecting them into a definite structure and meaning and thereby surpassing them' (*Nachlass*, vol. I, p. 114).

11. Cf. Marx, *Capital* (Moscow, 1961), vol. I, pp. 372–3n, where Marx, in discussing the history of religion, describes the method he advances as 'the only materialist and therefore scientific method'. More details on this will be given later.

almost impossible for it to make anything 'philosophical' out of a phenomenon like Marx's scientific socialism.

In the normal presentations of the history of the nineteenth-century philosophy which emanate from bourgeois authors, there is a gap at a specific point which can only be overcome in a highly artificial manner, if at all. These historians want to present the development of philosophical thought in a totally ideological and hopelessly undialectical way, as a pure process of the 'history of ideas'. It is therefore impossible to see how they can find a rational explanation for the fact that by the 1850s Hegel's grandiose philosophy had virtually no followers left in Germany and was totally misunderstood soon afterwards, whereas as late as the 1830s even its greatest enemies (Schopenhauer or Herbart) were unable to escape its overpowering intellectual influence. Most of them did not even try to provide such an explanation, but were instead content to note in their annals the disputes following Hegel's death under the utterly negative rubric of 'The Decay of Hegelianism'. Yet the content of these disputes was very significant and they were also, by today's standards, of an extremely high formal philosophical level. They took place between the various tendencies of Hegel's school, the Right, the Centre and the different tendencies of the Left, especially Strauss, Bauer, Feuerbach, Marx and Engels. To close this period, these historians of philosophy simply set a kind of absolute 'end' to the Hegelian philosophic movement. They then begin the 1860s with the return to Kant (Helmholtz, Zeller, Liebmann, Lange) which appears as a new epoch of philosophical development, without any direct connection to anything else. This kind of history of philosophy has three great limitations, two of which can be revealed by a critical revision that itself remains more or less completely within the realm of the history of ideas. Indeed, in recent years more thorough philosophers, especially Dilthey and his school, have considerably expanded the limited perspective of normal histories of philosophy in these two respects. These two limits can therefore be regarded as having been overcome in principle, although in practice they have survived to this day and will presumably continue to do so for a very long time. The third limit, however, cannot in any way be surpassed from within the realm of the history of ideas; consequently it has not yet been overcome even in principle by contemporary bourgeois historians of philosophy.

The first of these three limits in the bourgeois history of philosophy during the second half of the nineteenth century can be characterized as a 'purely philosophical' one. The ideologues of the time did not see that the ideas contained in a philosophy can live on not only in philosophies, but equally well in positive sciences and social practice, and that this process precisely began on a large scale with Hegel's philosophy. The second limit is a 'local' one, and was most typical of German professors of philosophy in the second half of the last century: these worthy Germans ignored the fact that there were other 'philosophers' beyond the boundaries of Germany. Hence, with a few exceptions, they quite failed to see that the Hegelian system, although pronounced dead in Germany for decades, had continued to flourish in several foreign countries, not only in its content but also as a system and a method. In the development of the history of philosophy over recent decades, these first two limits to its perspective have in principle been overcome, and the picture painted above of the standard histories of philosophy since 1850 has of late undergone considerable improvement. However, bourgeois philosophers and historians are quite unable to overcome a third limitation on their historical outlook, because this would entail these 'bourgeois' philosophers and historians of philosophy abandoning the *bourgeois class standpoint* which constitutes the most essential *a priori* of their entire historical and philosophical science. For what appears as the purely 'ideal' development of philosophy in the nineteenth century can in fact only be fully and essentially grasped by relating it to the concrete historical development of bourgeois society as a whole. It is precisely this relation that bourgeois historians of philosophy, at their present stage of development, are incapable of studying scrupulously and impartially.

This explains why right up to the present day certain phases of the general development of philosophy in the nineteenth century have had to remain 'transcendent' for these bourgeois historians of philosophy. It also explains why there are still certain curious 'blank patches' on the maps of contemporary bourgeois histories of philosophy (already described in connection with the 'end' of the Hegelian movement in the 1840s and the empty space after it, before the 'reawakening' of philosophy in the 1860s). It also becomes intelligible why bourgeois histories of philosophy today no longer have any coherent grasp even of a period of German philosophy whose concrete essence they previously had succeeded in understanding. In other words, neither the development of philosophical thought *after* Hegel, nor the preceding evolution of philosophy *from* Kant *to* Hegel, can be understood as a mere chain of ideas. Any attempt to understand the full nature and meaning of this whole later period – normally referred to in history books as the epoch of 'German idealism' – will fail hopelessly so long as certain connections that are vital for its whole form and course are not registered, or are registered only superficially or belatedly. These are the connections between the 'intellectual movement' of the period and the 'revolutionary movement' that was contemporary with it.

In Hegel's *History of Philosophy* and other works there are passages describing the nature of the philosophy of his immediate predecessors – Kant, Fichte, and Schelling – which are valid for the whole period of so-called 'German idealism' including its crowning 'conclusion', the Hegelian system itself. They are also applicable to the later conflicts in the 1840s between the various Hegelian tendencies. Hegel wrote that in the philosophic systems of this fundamentally revolutionary epoch, 'revolution was lodged and expressed as if in the very form of their thought'.[12] Hegel's accompanying statements make it quite clear that he was not talking of what contemporary bourgeois historians of philosophy like to call a revolution in thought – a nice, quiet process that takes place in the pure realm of the study and far away from the crude realm of real struggles. The greatest thinker produced by bourgeois society in its revolutionary period regarded a 'revolution in the form of thought' as an objective component of the total social process of a real revolution.[13] 'Only two peoples, the German and the French – despite or precisely

12. Hegel, *Lectures on the Philosophy of History* (London, 1896), vol. 3, p. 409.

13. Kant also likes to use the expression 'revolution' in the realm of pure thought, but one should say that he means something much more concrete than the bourgeois Kantians of today. It should be related to Kant's many statements in the *Conflict of the Faculties* and elsewhere, on the real occurrence of the revolution: 'The revolution of an intellectually gifted people, such as the one we are witnessing today, arouses all onlookers (who are not themselves directly involved) to sympathize with it, in a way that approaches enthusiasm.' 'Such a phenomenon in the history of mankind is never forgotten.' 'This occurrence is too great, too interwoven with the interests of mankind, and its influence spreads too widely across the world, for peoples not to be reminded of it and aroused to attempt it again when the circumstances are propitious.' These and similar statements by Kant are collected in vol. I of *Politische Literatur der Deutschen im 18. Jahrhundert*, (1847!) ed. Geismar, pp. 121ff.

because of their contrasts – took part in this great epoch of world history, whose deepest essence is grasped by the philosophy of history. Other nations took no inward part in it: their governments and peoples merely played a political role. This principle swept Germany as thought, spirit and concept; in France it was unleashed in effective reality. What reality there was in Germany, however, appeared as a violent result of external conditions and as a reaction to them.'[14] A few pages further on, when presenting the philosophy of Kant, Hegel returns to the same theme: 'Rousseau already placed the Absolute in Freedom; Kant possesses the same principle, only in a more theoretical version. The French regard it from the point of view of will, for they have a proverb '*Il a la tête pres du bonnet*' (He is hot-headed). France has a sense of reality, of accomplishment, because ideas there are translated more directly into action; consequently men there have applied themselves practically to reality. However much freedom in itself is concrete, in France it was applied to reality in an undeveloped and abstract form; and to establish abstraction in reality is to destroy that reality. The fanaticism of freedom, when the people took possession of it, became terrible. In Germany the same principle aroused the interest of consciousness but was only developed in a theoretical manner. We have all kinds of commotions within us and about us; but through

14. Hegel, op. cit., p. 409. It is well enough known that Marx fully adopted and consciously developed this view of Hegel's on the division of roles between the Germans and the French within the general process of the bourgeois revolution. Cf. all his early writings which contain such formulations as: 'In politics the Germans have thought what other peoples have done', 'Germany has only shared the development of modern peoples through the abstract activity of thought', and therefore the fate of Germans in the real world has consisted in their 'sharing the restorations of modern peoples without participating in their revolutions' (all from the 'Introduction to the *Critique of Hegel's Philosophy of Right*,' in *On Religion*, pp. 49, 52, 43).

them all the German head prefers to let its sleeping cap sit quietly where it is and silently carries on its operations beneath it – Immanuel Kant was born in Königsberg in 1724', and so on. These passages from Hegel affirm a principle which renders intelligible the innermost nature of this great period of world history: the dialectical relation between philosophy and reality. Elsewhere Hegel formulated this principle in a more general way, when he wrote that every philosophy can be nothing but '*its own epoch comprehended in thought.*'[15] Essential in any event for a real understanding of the development of philosophical thought, this axiom becomes even more relevant for a revolutionary period of social evolution. Indeed, it is exactly this that explains the fate which irresistibly overtook the further development of philosophy and the historical study of philosophy by the *bourgeois class* in the nineteenth century. In the middle of the nineteenth century this class ceased to be revolutionary in its social *practice*, and by an inner necessity it thereby also lost the ability to comprehend in *thought* the true dialectical interrelation of ideas and real historical developments, above all of philosophy and revolution. In social practice, the revolutionary development of the bourgeoisie declined and halted in the middle of the nineteenth century. This process found its ideological expression in the apparent decline and end of philosophical development, on which bourgeois historians dwell to this day. A typical example of this kind of thinking is the comment of Überweg and Heinze, who begin the relevant section of their book by saying that philosophy found itself at this time 'in a state of general exhaustion', and 'increasingly lost its influence on cultural activity'. According to Überweg, this sad occurrence was due primarily to 'tendencies of psychological

15. Preface to the *Philosophy of Right* (Knox translation), p. 11.

revulsion', whereas all 'external moments' had only a 'secondary effect'. This famous bourgeois historian of philosophy 'explains' the character of these 'tendencies of psychological revulsion' to himself and his readers as follows: 'People became tired of both inflated idealism and of metaphysical speculation (!) and wanted spiritual nourishment that had more substance to it.' The philosophic developments of the nineteenth century appear at once in a totally different form (even from the standpoint of the history of ideas a more adequate one) if they are tackled resolutely and thoroughly with a dialectical method, even in the undeveloped and only partly conscious form in which Hegel used it – in other words in the form of Hegel's idealist dialectic as opposed to Marx's materialist dialectic.

Viewed in this perspective, the revolutionary movement in the realm of ideas, rather than abating and finally ceasing in the 1840s, merely underwent a deep and significant change of character. Instead of making an *exit*, classical German philosophy, the ideological expression of the revolutionary movement of the bourgeoisie, made a *transition* to a new science which henceforward appeared in the history of ideas as the general expression of the revolutionary movement of the proletariat: the theory of 'scientific socialism' first founded and formulated by Marx and Engels in the 1840s. Bourgeois historians of philosophy have hitherto either entirely ignored this essential and necessary relation between German idealism and Marxism, or they have only conceived and presented it inadequately and incoherently. To grasp it properly, it is necessary to abandon the normal abstract and ideological approach of modern historians of philosophy for an approach that need not be specifically Marxist but is just straightforwardly dialectical, in the Hegelian *and* Marxist sense. If we do this, we can see at once not only the interrelations between

German idealist philosophy and Marxism, but also their internal necessity. Since the Marxist system is the theoretical expression of the revolutionary movement of the proletariat, and German idealist philosophy is the theoretical expression of the revolutionary movement of the bourgeoisie, they must stand intelligently and historically (i.e. ideologically) in the same relation to each other as the revolutionary movement of the proletariat as a class stands to the revolutionary movement of the bourgeoisie, in the realm of social and political practice. There is one unified historical process of historical development in which an 'autonomous' proletarian class movement emerges from the revolutionary movement of the third estate, and the new materialist theory of Marxism 'autonomously' confronts bourgeois idealist philosophy. All these processes affect each other reciprocally. The emergence of Marxist theory is, in Hegelian-Marxist terms, only the 'other side' of the emergence of the real proletarian movement; it is both sides together that comprise the concrete totality of the historical process.

This dialectical approach enables us to grasp the four different trends we have mentioned – the revolutionary movement of the bourgeoisie, idealist philosophy from Kant to Hegel, the revolutionary class movement of the proletariat, and the materialist philosophy of Marxism – as four moments of a single historical process. This allows us to understand the real nature of the new science, theoretically formulated by Marx and Engels,[16] which forms the general expression of the independent revolutionary movement of the proletariat. This

16. See the famous passage in the *Communist Manifesto* which reformulates Hegel's conception of the dialectical interrelation of philosophy and reality; it is translated from the still somewhat mystified fashion in which it was expressed by Hegel (philosophy is its 'epoch comprehended in thought') into a rational form: 'The theoretical con-

materialist philosophy emerged from the most advanced systems of revolutionary bourgeois idealism; and it is now intelligible why bourgeois histories of philosophy had either to ignore it completely or could only understand its nature in a negative and – literally – inverted sense.[17] The essential practical aims of the proletarian movement cannot be realized within bourgeois society and the bourgeois State. Similarly, the philosophy of this bourgeois society is unable to understand the nature of the general propositions in which the revolutionary movement of the proletariat has found its inde-

---

clusions of the communists . . . are only general expressions of the real relations of an existing class struggle, of a historical movement that is going on before our eyes' (Marx and Engels, *Selected Works*, vol. I, p. 46).

17. 'A product of the collapse of Hegelian philosophy' (the prevailing view). 'The fall of the Titans of German idealism' (Plenge). 'An outlook that is rooted in the denial of values' (Schulze-Gavernitz). This view sees Marxism as an evil spirit that has fallen from the heights of German idealism into the bottomless depths of its materialist hell. The absurdity of this view is shown particularly clearly by the fact that those very aspects of Marxism in which are seen the effects of its fall were already contained in the systems of idealist bourgeois philosophy and were adopted by Marx without any apparent alteration. For example, the concept of evil as necessary for the development of the human race (Kant, Hegel); the concept of the necessary interconnection of increasing wealth and increasing poverty in bourgeois society (Hegel, *Philosophy of Right*, sections 243–5). These are the very forms through which the *bourgeois* class at its most developed stage had already acquired a certain consciousness of the class contradictions contained within it. Bourgeois consciousness made these contradictions absolute and therefore saw them as theoretically and practically *insoluble*. Marx superseded it because he no longer saw the contradictions as natural and absolute, but as historical and relative. They were therefore *capable of being abolished* in practice and theory by a higher form of social organization. In ignoring this, these bourgeois philosophers still conceive of Marxism itself in a narrow, negative and falsified bourgeois form.

pendent and self-conscious expression. The bourgeois standpoint has to stop in theory where it has to stop in social practice – as long as it does not want to cease being a 'bourgeois' standpoint altogether, in other words supersede itself. Only when the history of philosophy surmounts this barrier does scientific socialism cease to be a transcendental Beyond and become a possible object of comprehension. The peculiarity, however, that greatly complicates any correct understanding of the problem of 'Marxism and philosophy' is this: it appears as if in the very act of surpassing the limits of a bourgeois position – an act indispensable to grasp the essentialy new philosophical content of Marxism – *Marxism itself is at once superseded and annihilated as a philosophical object.*

At the outset of this investigation we stated that Marx and Engels, the founders of scientific socialism, were far from wanting to construct a new philosophy. In contrast to bourgeois thinkers, on the other hand, they were both fully aware of the close historical connection between their materialist theory and bourgeois idealist philosophy. According to Engels, socialism in its *content* is the product of *new* conceptions that necessarily arise at a definite stage of social development within the proletariat as a result of its material situation. But it created its own specific scientific *form* (which distinguishes it from utopian socialism) by its link with German idealism, especially the philosophical system of Hegel. Socialism, which developed from utopia to science, formally *emerged* from German idealist philosophy.[18] Naturally, this

18. Cf. Engels, *Anti-Dühring*, pp. 27, 37ff. On the fact that classical German philosophy was even in theory not the *only* source of scientific socialism, see Engels's remark in the note added to the preface to the first edition of *Socialism: Utopian and Scientific*; see also his remarks on Fourier's fragment *On Trade* (*Nachlass*, II, pp. 407ff.).

(formal) philosophical *origin* did not mean that socialism therefore had to remain a philosophy in its *independent form* and *further development*. From 1845 onwards, at the latest, Marx and Engels characterized their new materialist and scientific standpoint as no longer philosophical.[19] It should be remembered here that all philosophy was for them equivalent to bourgeois philosophy. But it is precisely the significance of this equation of all philosophy with bourgeois philosophy that needs to be stressed. For it involves much the same relationship as that of Marxism and the State. Marx and Engels not only combatted one specific historical form of the State, but historically and materialistically they equated the State as such with the bourgeois State and they therefore declared the abolition of the State to be the political aim of communism. Similarly, they were not just combatting specific philosophical systems – they wanted eventually to overcome and supersede philosophy altogether, by scientific socialism.[20] It is here that

19. Marx's *Theses on Feuerbach*, to be discussed later, date from this year. It was then too that Marx and Engels (see Marx's account in the 1859 Preface to the *Critique of Political Economy*) abandoned their 'previous' philosophical outlook by carrying out a critique of the whole of post-Hegelian philosophy (*The German Ideology*). From then on the purpose of their polemics on philosophical questions is only to enlighten or annihilate their opponents (such as Proudhon, Lassalle and Dühring); it is no longer intended to 'clarify their own position'.

20. See, first of all, the relevant passage from the *Communist Manifesto* (*Selected Works*, vol. I, pp. 52–3). '"Undoubtedly," it will be said, "religious, moral, philosophical and juridical ideas have been modified in the course of historical development. But religion, morality, philosophy, political, science, and law, constantly survived this change." "There are also eternal truths, such as freedom, justice, etc., that are common to all states of society. But communism abolishes eternal truths; it abolishes all religion, and all morality, instead of constituting them on a new basis. It therefore acts in contradiction to all past historical experience." What does this accusation reduce itself to? The history of all past society has consisted in the development of class

we find the major contradiction between the 'realistic' (i.e. dialectically materialist) conception of Marxism and the 'ideological humbug of jurists and others' (Marx) characteristic of Lassalleanism and all earlier and later versions of 'vulgar socialism'. The latter basically never surpassed the 'bourgeois level', i.e. the standpoint of 'bourgeois society'.[21]

Any thorough elucidation of the relationship between 'Marxism and philosophy' must start from the unambiguous statements of Marx and Engels themselves that a necessary result of their new dialectical-materialist standpoint was the supersession, not only of bourgeois idealist philosophy, but *simultaneously* of all philosophy *as such*.[22] It is essential not

---

antagonisms, antagonisms that assumed different forms at different epochs.

But whatever form they may have taken, one fact is common to all past ages: the exploitation of one part of society by the other. No wonder, then, that the social consciousness of past ages, despite all the multiplicity and variety it displaces, moves within certain common forms, in forms of consciousness which cannot completely disappear without the total disappearance of class antagonisms.

The communist revolution is the most radical rupture with traditional property relations; no wonder that its development involves the most radical rupture with traditional ideas.' The relationship of Marxism to philosophy or religion is thus basically similar to its relationship to the fundamental economic ideology of bourgeois society and the fetishism of commodities or value. Cf. – for the moment – *Capital*, vol. I, pp. 75ff., especially p. 80n. and p. 81n. and Marx's 1875 *Critique of the Gotha Programme* (Marx and Engels, *Selected Works*, vol. II, pp. 29ff. [value], pp. 31ff. [the state] and p. 35 [religion]).

21. See Marx's *Critique of the Gotha Programme* (*passim*).

22. See, e.g., Engels's point in *Ludwig Feuerbach* (*Selected Works*, vol. II, p. 365) which sounds somewhat ideological in the way it is expressed: 'At any rate, with Hegel philosophy comes to an end. On the one hand, because in his system he summed up its whole development in its most splendid fashion; and on the other, because, even though unconsciously, he showed us the way out of the labyrinth of systems to real positive knowledge of the world.'

to obscure the fundamental significance of this Marxist attitude towards philosophy by regarding the whole dispute as a purely verbal one – implying that Engels simply bestowed a new name on certain epistemological principles known in Hegelian terminology as 'the philosophical aspect of sciences', which were, substantially preserved in the materialist transformation of the Hegelian dialectic.[23] There are, of course, some formulations in Marx and especially the later Engels[24] which appear to suggest this. But it is easy to see that philosophy itself is not abolished by a mere abolition of its name.[25] Such purely terminological points must be dismissed in any serious examination of the relationship between Marxism and

23. There really are bourgeois and even (vulgar) Marxist theoreticians who seriously imagine that when Marxist communists demand the abolition of *the State* (as distinct from opposition to specific historical forms of the State), there is only a terminological difference involved.

24. Cf. especially *Anti-Dühring*, pp. 34–40, and *Ludwig Feuerbach*, op. cit., pp. 400–1. The formulations in both passages have the same content, and the quotation here is from *Anti-Dühring*, pp. 39–40: 'In both cases (i.e. in relation to both history and nature) modern materialism is essentially dialectical, and no longer needs any philosophy standing above the other sciences. As soon as each individual science is bound to make clear its position in the great totality of things, a special science dealing with this totality is superfluous. That which still survives independently of all earlier philosophy is the science of thought and its laws – formal logic and dialectics. Everything else is subsumed in the positive science of nature and history.'

25. In the form in which they are quoted here, Engels's statements clearly contain no more than a change of name. There appears to be no fundamental difference between what Engels alleges are the consequences of the Marxist or materialist dialectics, and what follows anyway from Hegel's dialectics, and what Hegel has already stated to be the consequences of his dialectical idealist position. Even Hegel demands that every science make clear its place in a general context; he then continues along the following lines: it follows that every true science is necessarily philosophical. Verbally what this entails is the opposite of Engels's transformation of philosophy into science; but in essence they would both appear to mean the same thing. Both want to

philosophy. The problem is rather how we should understand the abolition of philosophy of which Marx and Engels spoke – mainly in the 1840s, but on many later occasions as well. *How* should this process be accomplished, or has it already been accomplished? By what actions? At what speed? And for whom? Should this abolition of philosophy be regarded as accomplished so to speak once and for all by a single intellectual deed of Marx and Engels? Should it be regarded as accomplished only for Marxists, or for the whole proletariat, or for the whole of humanity?[26] Or should we see it (like the abolition of the State) as a very long and arduous revolutionary process which unfolds through the most

---

abolish the contradiction between individual sciences and a philosophy that stands above them. Hegel expresses this by incorporating individual sciences within philosophy; whereas Engels dissolves philosophy in the individual sciences. In both cases this would seem to have the same result: the individual sciences cease to be specific sciences, and at the same time philosophy ceases to be a special science standing above others. Later on, however, it will be shown that there is more behind what appears here to be a purely verbal difference between Hegel and Engels. This difference is not as clearly expressed in these statements of Engels, and above all in his later formulations, as it is in the earlier works that Marx wrote alone or with Engels. What is important in this context is that although he is always avoiding 'positive science', Engels still wants to preserve the independence of a definite, limited area within 'philosophy' (the theory of thought and its laws – formal logic and dialectics). The important question this raises is, of course, what Marx and Engels really mean by the concept of science or positive science.

26. It will be shown later that even some excellent materialist thinkers have unfortunately come near to adopting this extremely ideological view. Moreover, the statement by Engels quoted above (note 24) can be interpreted to mean that in essence philosophy had already been intellectually overcome and superseded by Hegel himself, unconsciously, and was then consciously superseded with the discovery of the materialistic principle. However, we shall see that despite appearances *the way Engels expresses this* does not convey the real *meaning* of Marx's and Engels's conception.

diverse phases? If so, what is the relationship of Marxism to philosophy so long as this arduous process has not yet attained its final goal, the abolition of philosophy?

If the question of the relationship of Marxism to philosophy is posed like this, it becomes clear that we are not dealing with senseless and pointless reflections on issues that have long been resolved. On the contrary, the problem remains of the greatest theoretical and practical importance. Indeed, it is especially crucial in the present stage of the proletarian class struggle. Orthodox Marxists behaved for many decades as if no problem was involved at all, or at most only one which would always remain immaterial to the practice of the class struggle. It is now this position itself which appears highly dubious – all the more so in the light of the peculiar parallelism between the two problems of Marxism and Philosophy and Marxism and State. It is well known that the latter, as Lenin says in *State and Revolution*,[27] 'hardly concerned the major theoreticians and publicists of the Second International'. This raises the question: if there is a definite connection between the abolition of the State and the abolition of the philosophy, is there also a connection between the neglect of these two problems by the Marxists of the Second International? The problem can be posed more exactly. Lenin's bitter criticism of the debasement of Marxism by opportunism connects the neglect of the problem of the State by the Marxists of the Second International to a more general context. Is this context also operative in the case of Marxism and philosophy? In other words, is the neglect of the problem of philosophy by the Marxists of the Second International also related to the fact that '*problems of revolution in general hardly concerned them*'?

27. *State and Revolution*, Chapter 6, 'The Vulgarization of Marx by the Opportunists', Lenin, *Collected Works*, vol. 25.

To clarify the matter, we must make a more detailed analysis of the nature and causes of the greatest crisis that has yet occurred in the history of Marxist theory and which in the last decade has split Marxists into three hostile camps.

At the beginning of the twentieth century, the long period of purely evolutionary development of capitalism came to an end, and a new epoch of revolutionary struggle began. Because of this change in the practical conditions of class struggle, there were increasing signs that Marxist theory had entered a critical phase. It became obvious that the extraordinarily banal and rudimentary vulgar-marxism of the epigones had an extremely inadequate awareness of even the totality of its own problems, let alone any definite positions on a whole range of questions outside them. The crisis of Marxist theory showed itself most clearly in the problem of the attitude of social revolution towards the State. This major issue had never been seriously posed in practice since the defeat of the first proletarian revolutionary movement in 1848, and the repression of the revolt of the Commune of 1871. It was put concretely on the agenda once again by the World War, the first and second Russian Revolutions of 1917, and the collapse of the Central Powers in 1918. It now became clear that there was no unanimity whatever within the camp of Marxism on such major issues of transition and goal as the 'seizure of State power by the proletariat', the 'dictatorship of the proletariat', and the final 'withering away of the State' in communist society. On the contrary, no sooner were all these questions posed in a concrete and unavoidable manner, than there emerged at least three different theoretical positions on them, all of which claimed to be Marxist. Yet in the pre-war period, the most prominent representatives of these three tendencies – respectively Renner, Kautsky and Lenin – had not only been regarded as Marxists but as orthodox Marxists.[28] For some decades there had been an apparent crisis in the camp of the Social Democrat parties and trade unions of the Second International; this took the shape of a conflict between orthodox Marxism and revisionism.[29] But with the emergence of different socialist tendencies over these new questions, it became clear that this apparent crisis was only a provisional and illusory version of a much deeper rift that ran through the orthodox Marxist front itself. On one side of this rift, there appeared Marxist neo-reformism which soon more or less amalgamated with the earlier revisionism. On the other side, the theoretical representatives of a new revolutionary proletarian party unleashed a struggle against both the old reformism of the revisionists and the new reformism of the 'Centre', under the battle-cry of restoring pure or revolutionary Marxism.

This crisis erupted within the Marxist camp at the outbreak of the World War. But it would be an extremely superficial and undialectical conception of the historical process – thoroughly non-Marxist and non-materialist, indeed not even Hegeliano-idealist - to attribute it merely to the cowardice, or deficient revolutionary convictions, of the theoreticians and publicists who were responsible for this impoverishment and reduction of Marxist theory to the orthodox vulgar-marxism of the Second International. Yet it would be equally superficial and undialectical to imagine that the great polemics

28. For information on how these theories first conflicted with each other in the World War, see Renner, *Marxizmus, Krieg und Internationale*; Kautsky's attack on Renner, *Kriegssozialismus* in *Marx-Studien*, Vienna, IV, 1; and Lenin's polemics against Renner, Kautsky and others, in *State and Revolution* and *Against the Stream*.

29. Cf. Kautsky, 'Three Crises in Marxism', in *Neue Zeit*, 21, I (1903) pp. 723ff.

between Lenin, Kautsky and other 'Marxists' were merely intended to restore Marxism, by faithfully re-establishing the Marxist doctrine.[30] Hitherto we have only used the dialectical method, which Hegel and Marx introduced into the study of history, to analyse the philosophy of German idealism and the Marxist theory that *emerged* from it. But the only really 'materialist and therefore scientific method' (Marx) of pursuing this analysis is to apply it to the *further development* of Marxism up to the present. This means that we must try to understand every change, development and revision of

30. Those who approach Lenin's writings without a deeper understanding of their practical and theoretical context might think that Lenin had in fact adopted such a moralistic, psychological and ideological position of a bourgeois kind. What might mislead them is the extremely bitter and personal way in which Lenin (in this respect a faithful disciple of Marx) attacks 'vulgar-marxism' as well as the textual erudition and precision with which Lenin uses the writings of Marx and Engels. A careful reading shows quite clearly, however, that Lenin never invokes personal factors to explain the process that had been developing internationally for decades, and through which Marxist theory in the second half of the nineteenth century became gradually impoverished and degenerated into vulgar-marxism. He confines his use of this factor to explaining a few specific historical phenomena in the last period just before the World War, when the imminent political and social crisis was clear. It would also be a great distortion of Marxism to claim that Lenin thought that accidents and personal peculiarities were of no significance for the history of the world or for explaining specific historical phenomena (cf. Marx's famous letter to Kugelmann, 17 April 1871, in Marx and Engels, *Selected Correspondence*, Moscow, n.d., pp. 319–20) and the general point on the 'justification of accident' in the aphoristic final part of the 1857 Introduction to the *Critique of Political Economy*, English translation, Chicago, 1904, p. 309). On the other hand, according to Marxist theory, the personal factor must naturally play a less important explanatory role, the longer the periods which the explanation is supposed to cover. One can easily see that in all his writings Lenin always worked in this genuine 'materialist' way. But the preface and first page of *State and Revolution* prove that he was also just as far from considering the main purpose of this theoretical work to be the ideological 're-establishment' of true Marxist doctrine.

Marxist theory, since its original emergence from the philosophy of German Idealism, as a necessary product of its epoch (Hegel). More precisely, we should seek to understand their determination by the totality of the historico-social process of which they are a general expression (Marx). We will then be able to grasp the real origins of the degeneration of Marxist theory into vulgar-marxism. We may also discern the meaning of the passionate yet apparently 'ideological' efforts of the Marxist theorists of the Third International today to restore 'Marx's genuine doctrine'.

If we thus apply Marx's principle of dialectical materialism to the whole history of Marxism, we can distinguish three major stages of development through which Marxist theory has passed *since* its birth – inevitably so in the context of the concrete social development of this epoch. The first phase begins around 1843, and corresponds in the history of ideas to the *Critique of Hegel's Philosophy of Right*. It ends with the Revolution of 1848 – corresponding to the *Communist Manifesto*. The second phase begins with the bloody suppression of the Parisian proletariat in the battle of June 1848 and the resultant crushing of all the working class's organizations and dreams of emancipation 'in a period of feverish industrial activity, moral degeneration and political reaction', as Marx masterfully describes it in his *Inaugural Address* of 1864. We are not concerned here with the social history of the working-class as a whole, but only with the internal development of Marxist theory in its relation to the general class history of the proletariat. Hence the second period may be said to last approximately to the end of the century, leaving out all the less important divisions (the foundation and collapse of the First International; the interlude of the Commune; the struggle between Marxists and Lassalleaner; the Anti-socialist laws in Germany; trade unions; the founding of the Second

International). The third phase extends from the start of this century to the present and into an indefinite future.

Arranged in this way, the historical development of Marxist theory presents the following picture. The first manifestation of it naturally remained essentially unchanged in the minds of Marx and Engels themselves throughout the later period, although in their *writings* it did not stay entirely unaltered. In spite of all their denials of philosophy, this first version of the theory is permeated through and through with philosophical thought. It is a theory of *social development* seen and comprehended as a living totality; or, more precisely, it is a theory of *social revolution* comprehended and practised as a living totality. At this stage there is no question whatever of dividing the economic, political and intellectual moments of this totality into separate branches of knowledge, even while every concrete peculiarity of each separate moment is comprehended analysed and criticized with historical fidelity. Of course, it is not only economics, politics and ideology, but also the historical process and conscious social action that continue to make up the living unity of 'revolutionary practice' (*Theses on Feuerbach*). The best example of this early and youthful form of Marxist theory as the theory of social revolution is obviously the *Communist Manifesto.*[31]

It is wholly understandable from the viewpoint of the materialist dialectic that this original form of Marxist theory could not subsist unaltered throughout the long years of the second half of the nineteenth century (which was in practice quite unrevolutionary). Marx's remark in the *Preface to the Critique of Political Economy* on mankind as a whole is neces-

31. But later writings such as *The Class Struggles in France* and *The Eighteenth Brumaire of Louis Bonaparte* also belong historically to this phase.

sarily also true for the working class, which was then slowly and antagonistically maturing towards its own liberation: 'It always sets itself only such problems as it can solve; since, looking at the matter more closely it will always be found that the problem itself arises only when the material conditions for its solution are already present or are at least understood to be in the process of emergence'. This dictum is not affected by the fact that a problem which supersedes present relations may have been formulated in an anterior epoch. To accord theory an autonomous existence outside the objective movement of history would obviously be neither materialist, nor dialectical in the Hegelian sense; it would simply be an idealist metaphysic. A dialectical conception comprehends every form without exception in terms of the flow of this movement, and it necessarily follows from it that Marx's and Engels's theory of social revolution inevitably underwent considerable changes in the course of its further development. When Marx in 1864 drafted the *Inuagural Address* and the *Statutes of the First International* he was perfectly conscious of the fact that 'time was needed for the reawakened movement to permit the old audacity of language'.[32] This is of course true not only for language but for all the other components of the theory of the movement. Therefore the scientific socialism of the *Capital* of 1867–94 and the other later writings of Marx and Engels represent an expression of the general theory of Marxism, which is in many ways a different and more developed one

32. Marx and Engels, *Selected Correspondence*, p. 182 [4 November 1864]. This passage is of great importance for a concrete interpretation of the *Inaugural Address*, yet it is significantly omitted by Kautsky when he quotes large parts of the letter in the preface to his 1922 edition of the *Briefwechsel* (pp. 4–5). Having thus toned down the 1864 *Inaugural Address* he is able (ibid. p. 11ff.) to play it off against the fiery style of the 1847–8 *Communist Manifesto*, and against the 'illegal agents of the Third International'.

than that of the direct revolutionary communism of the *Manifesto* of 1847–8 – or for that matter, *The Poverty of Philosophy, The Class Struggles in France* and *The Eighteenth Brumaire.* Nevertheless, the central characteristic of Marxist theory remains essentially unaltered even in the later writings of Marx and Engels. For in its later version, as scientific socialism, the Marxism of Marx and Engels remains the inclusive whole of a theory of social revolution. The difference is only that in the later phase the various components of this whole, its economic, political and ideological elements, scientific theory and social practice, are further separated out. We can use an expression of Marx's and say that the umbilical cord of its natural combination has been broken. In Marx and Engels, however, this never produces a multiplicity of independent elements instead of the whole. It is merely that another combination of the components of the system emerges developed with greater scientific precision and built on the infrastructure of the critique of political economy. In the writings of its creators, the Marxist system itself never dissolves into a sum of separate branches of knowledge, in spite of a practical and outward employment of its results that suggests such a conclusion. For example, many bourgeois interpreters of Marx and some later Marxists thought they were able to distinguish between the historical and the theoretico-economic material in Marx's major work *Capital*; but all they proved by this is that they understood nothing of the real method of Marx's critique of political economy. For it is one of the essential signs of his dialectical materialist method that this distinction does not exist for it; it is indeed precisely a theoretical comprehension of history. Moreover, the unbreakable interconnection of theory and practice, which formed the most characteristic sign of the first communist version of Marx's materialism, was in no way abolished in the later form of his system. It is only to the superficial glance that a pure theory of thought seems to have displaced the practice of the revolutionary will. This revolutionary will is latent, yet present, in every sentence of Marx's work and erupts again and again in every decisive passage, especially in the first volume of *Capital.* One need only think of the famous seventh section of Chapter 24 on the historical tendency of capital accumulation.[33]

On the other hand, it has to be said that the supporters and followers of Marx, despite all their theoretical and methodological avowals of historical materialism, in fact divided the theory of social revolution into fragments. The correct materialist conception of history, understood theoretically in a dialectical way and practically in a revolutionary way, is incompatible with separate branches of knowledge that are isolated and autonomous, and with purely theoretical investigations that are scientifically objective in dissociation from revolutionary practice. Yet later Marxists came to regard scientific socialism more and more as a set of purely scientific observations, without any *immediate* connection to the political or other practices of class struggle. Sufficient proof of this is one writer's account of the relation between Marxist science and politics, who was in the best sense a representative Marxist theoretician of the Second International. In December 1909, Rudolph Hilferding published his *Finance Capital* which

33. There are other good examples of this at the end of Chapter 8, on the Working Day (*Capital,* vol. 1, Moscow, 1961, p. 302): 'For protection against the serpent of their agonies, the labourers must put their heads together, and, as a class, compel the passing of a law.' See also the famous passage (*Capital,* vol. 3, part II) where Marx returns to this theme. There are so many other similar places in *Capital* that there is no need to refer to such directly revolutionary writings of the later period as the Address to the General Council of the First International on the revolt of the Paris Commune (*The Civil War in France,* 1871).

attempts to 'understand scientifically' the economic aspects of the most recent development of capitalism 'by inserting these phenomena into the theoretical system of classical political economy'. In the introduction he wrote: 'Here it need only be said that for Marxism the study of politics itself aims only at the discovery of causal connections. Knowledge of the laws governing a society of commodity production reveals at once the determinants of the will of the classes of this society. For a Marxist, the task of scientific politics – a politics which describes causal connections – is to discover these determinants of the will of classes. Marxist politics, like Marxist theory, is free of value-judgements. It is therefore false simply to identify Marxism with socialism, although it is very common for Marxists and non-Marxists to do so. Logically Marxism, seen only as a scientific system and therefore apart from its historical effects, is only a theory of the laws of motion of society, which the Marxist conception of history formulated in general, while Marxist economics has applied it to the age of commodity production. The advent of socialism is a result of tendencies that develop in a society that produces commodities. But insight into the correctness of Marxism, which includes insight into the necessity of socialism, is in no way a result of value judgements and has no implications for practical behaviour. It is one thing to acknowledge a necessity and quite another to place oneself at the service of this necessity. It is more than possible that a man may be convinced of the final victory of socialism, and yet decides to fight against it. The insight into the laws of motion of society provided by Marxism ensures superiority to whoever has mastered them. The most dangerous opponents of socialism are undoubtedly those who have profited most from its experience.' According to Hilferding, Marxism is a theory which is logically 'a scientific, objective and free science, without value judgements'. He has no difficulty in explaining the remarkable fact that people so often identify it with the struggle for socialism by invoking the 'insuperable reluctance of the ruling class to accept the results of Marxism' and therefore to take the 'trouble' to study such a 'complicated system'. 'Only in this sense is it the science of the proletariat and the opponent of bourgeois economics, since it otherwise holds unflinchingly to the claim made by every science of the objective and general validity of its conclusions'.[34] Thus the materialist conception of history, which in Marx and Engels was essentially a dialectical one, eventually become something quite undialectical in their epigones. For one tendency, it has changed into a kind of heuristic principle of specialized theoretical investigation. For another, the fluid methodology of Marx's materialist dialectic freezes into a number of theoretical formulations about the causal interconnection of historical phenomena in different areas of society – in other words it became something that could best be described as a general systematic sociology. The former school treated Marx's materialist principle as merely a 'subjective basis for

34. Up to 1914 or 1918 a proletarian reader might have thought that Hilferding and other orthodox Marxists who said such things, and who claimed that their writings had objective and universal validity (i.e. independent of any class basis), had done so out of practical and tactical considerations in the interests of the working class. But their subsequent practice has demonstrated beyond any doubt the error of this interpretation. The example of Marxists like Paul Lensch shows that this kind of 'scientific knowledge' can be used 'perfectly well' *against* socialism. In this connection one can also mention that Hilferding's distinction between Marxism and Socialism, criticized here, is taken to its most absurd conclusions by Simkhovitch, a bourgeois critic of Marx, in his *Marxism against Socialism* (London, 1913). The book is original and interesting for this reason alone; it was comprehensively reviewed by M. Rubinov, 'Marx's Prophecies in the Light of Modern Statistics' in Grünberg's *Archiv für die Geschichte des Sozialismus und der Arbeiterbewegung*, VI, pp. 129–56.

reflective judgement'[35] in Kant's sense, while the latter dogmatically regarded the teachings of Marxist 'sociology' primarily as an economic system, or even a geographical and biological one.[36] All these deformations and a row of other less important ones were inflicted on Marxism by its epigones in the second phase of its development, and they can be summarized in one all-inclusive formulation: a unified general theory of social revolution was changed into criticisms of the bourgeois economic order, of the bourgeois State, of the bourgeois system of education, of bourgeois religion, art, science and culture. These criticisms no longer necessarily

35. Cf. *Critique of Judgement* (Barnard translation 1914; section 75, pp. 309–10). In the same passage Kant describes this maxim as a 'guiding thread for the study of nature'; similarly Marx in the Preface to the *Critique of Political Economy* describes the passage which lays out his materialist conception as a 'guiding thread' for further study, which is derived from his philosophical and scientific investigations. One could then claim that Marx had referred to his materialist principle as a mere guide for studying society, in the way that Kant's critical philosophy was a guide. One could also cite as further examples all the statements in which Marx defends himself against critics who claim that his *Critique of Political Economy* contained *a priori* elements or a theory that was abstract, supra-historical and influenced by the philosophy of history. (See the postscript to the second German edition of *Capital*-1873, op. cit., vol. I, pp. 17–18, and the well-known letter to Mikhailovsky of November 1877, *Selected Correspondence*, pp. 376ff.) However, it has already been made clear in my early work, *Kernpunkte der materialistischen Geschichtsauffassung* (Berlin, 1922), why it is inadequate to regard Marx's materialist principle as a purely heuristic one (Cf. especially pp. 16ff. and the first two appendices).

36. See in particular the preface to my *Kernpunkte* and the criticisms there of Ludwig Woltmann, pp. 18ff. There are some modern Marxist theoreticians who belong in practice to revolutionary communism, but who come near to equating the Marxist conception of history with a 'general sociology'. Cf. Bukharin, *Historical Materialism* (Ann Arbor Paperback, 1969), pp. 13–14, and K. Wittfogel, *Die Wissenschaft der bürgerlichen Gesellschaft* (1922), p. 50.

develop by their very nature into revolutionary practice;[37] they can equally well develop, into all kinds of attempts at *reform*, which fundamentally remain within the limits of bourgeois society and the bourgeois State, and in actual practice usually did so. This distortion of the revolutionary doctrine of Marxism itself – into a purely theoretical critique that no longer leads to practical revolutionary action, or does so only haphazardly – is very clear if one compares the *Communist Manifesto* or even the 1864 *Statutes of the First International* drawn up by Marx, to the programmes of the Socialist Parties of Central and Western Europe in the second half of the nineteenth century, and especially to that of the German Social Democratic Party. It is well known how bitterly critical Marx and Engels were of the fact that German Social Democracy made almost entirely *reformist* demands in the political as well as cultural and ideological fields in their Gotha (1875) and Erfurt (1891) programmes. These documents contained not a whiff of the genuine materialist and revolutionary principle in Marxism.[38] Indeed, towards the end of the century this situation led to the assaults of revisionism on orthodox Marxism. Eventually, at the start of the twentieth century, the first signs of the approaching storm heralded a new period of conflicts and revolutionary battles, and thereby led to the

37. Cf. Marx, 'Introduction to the *Critique of Hegel's Philosophy of Right*', in Marx and Engels, *On Religion*, pp. 50ff., where Marx says that criticism of the modern State, of the reality that is related to it, and of all previous German political and legal consciousness should debouch into a practice '*à la hauteur des principes*' – i.e. in a revolution, and not a 'partial, merely political revolution', but a revolution by the proletariat, which emancipates not only political man but the whole of social man.

38. See the statements by Marx and Engels on the Gotha Programme collected in my edition of Marx's *Critique of the Gotha Programme* (Berlin, 1922; also in Marx and Engels *Selected Works*, vol. II, pp. 13ff.) and also Engels's 'Notes on the Erfurt Programme', *Neue Zeit*, 20, I, pp. 5ff.

decisive crisis of Marxism in which we still find ourselves today.

Both processes may be seen as necessary phases of a total ideological and material development – once it is understood that the decline of the original Marxist theory of social revolution into a theoretical critique of society without any revolutionary consequences is for dialectical materialism a necessary expression of parallel changes in the social practice of the proletarian struggle. Revisionism appears as an attempt to express in the form of a coherent theory the reformist character acquired by the economic struggles of the trade unions and the political struggles of the working class parties, under the influence of altered historical conditions. The so-called orthodox Marxism of this period (now a mere vulgar-marxism) appears largely as an attempt by theoreticians, weighed down by tradition, to maintain the theory of social revolution which formed the first version of Marxism, in the shape of pure theory. This theory was wholly abstract and had no practical consequences – it merely sought to reject the new reformist theories, in which the real character of the historical movement was then expressed as un-Marxist. This is precisely why, in a new revolutionary period, it was the orthodox Marxists of the Second International who were inevitably the least able to cope with such questions as the relation between the State and proletarian revolution. The revisionists at least possessed a theory of the relationship of the 'working people' to the State, although this theory was in no way a Marxist one. Their theory and practice had long since substituted political, social and cultural reforms within the bourgeois State for a social revolution that would seize, smash and replace it by the dictatorship of the proletariat. The orthodox Marxists were content to reject this solution to the problems of the transitional period as a violation of the principles of Marxism. Yet with all their orthodox obsession with the abstract letter of Marxist theory they were unable to preserve its original revolutionary character. Their scientific socialism itself had inevitably ceased to be a theory of social revolution. Over a long period, when Marxism was slowly spreading throughout Europe, it had in fact no practical revolutionary task to accomplish. Therefore problems of revolution had ceased, even in theory, to exist as problems of the real world for the great majority of Marxists, orthodox as well as revisionist. As far as the reformists were concerned, these problems had disappeared completely. But even for the orthodox Marxists they had wholly lost the immediacy with which the authors of the *Manifesto* had confronted them, and receded into a distant and eventually quite transcendental *future.*[39] In this period people became used to pursuing here and now policies of which revisionism may be seen as the theoretical expression. Officially condemned by party congresses, this revisionism was in the end accepted no less officially by the trade unions. At the beginning of the century, a new period of development put the question of social revolution back on the agenda as a realistic and terrestrial question in all its vital dimensions. Therewith purely theoretical orthodox Marxism – till the outbreak of the World War the officially established version of Marxism in the Second International – collapsed completely and disintegrated. This was, of course, an inevitable result of its long internal decay.[40] It is in this epoch that we can see in many countries the beginnings

39. Cf. the passage from Kautsky's attack on Bernstein, *Bernstein und das Sozialdemokratische Programm*, p. 172, which Lenin criticized in *State and Revolution* (*Collected Works*, vol. 25): 'We can just as well *postpone to a future date* any decision on the problem of the dictatorship of the proletariat.'

40. Cf. the 'alteration' of Marx's theory of the dictatorship, contained in Kautsky's latest work, *Die proletarische Revolution und ihr Programm*, 1922 (*Translator's Note*: published in English under the

of *third period of development*, above all represented by Russian Marxists, and often described by its major representatives as a 'restoration' of Marxism.

This transformation and development of Marxist theory has been effected under the peculiar ideological guise of a return to the pure teaching of original or true Marxism. Yet it is easy to understand both the reasons for this guise and the real character of the process which is concealed by it. What theoreticians like Rosa Luxemburg in Germany and Lenin in Russia have done, and are doing, in the field of Marxist theory is to liberate it from the inhibiting traditions of the Social Democracy of the second period. They thereby answer the practical needs of the new revolutionary stage of proletarian class struggle, for these traditions weighed 'like a nightmare' on the brain of the working masses whose objectively revolutionary socio-economic position no longer corresponded to these evolutionary doctrines.[41] The apparent revival of original Marxist theory in the Third International is simply a result of the fact that in a new revolutionary period not only the workers' movement itself, but the theoretical conceptions of communists which express it, must assume an explicitly

---

title *The Labour Revolution*, 1926): 'In his famous article criticizing the Social Democratic Party's programme Marx says: "*Between capitalist and communist society, there lies the period of the revolutionary transformation of the one into the other. Corresponding to this is a period of political transition in which the state can be nothing but the revolutionary dictatorship of the proletariat.*" Given our experiences over the last few years we can now *alter* this passage on the kind of government we want, and say: "*Between the period of a purely bourgeois state and a purely proletarian state, there lies a period of the transformation of one into the other. Corresponding to this there is also a period of political transition, in which the state will usually take the form of a coalition government*" ' (*The Labour Revolution*, pp. 53–4).

41. Marx, *The Eighteenth Brumaire, Selected Works*, vol. I, pp. 247ff.

revolutionary form. This is why large sections of the Marxist system, which seemed virtually forgotten in the final decades of the nineteenth century, have now come to life again. It also explains why the leader of the Russian Revolution could write a book a few months before October in which he stated that his aim was 'in the first place to *restore* the correct Marxist theory of the State'. Events themselves placed the question of the dictatorship of the proletariat on the agenda as a practical problem. When Lenin placed the same question theoretically on the agenda at a decisive moment, this was an early indication that the internal connection of theory and practice within revolutionary Marxism had been consciously re-established.[42]

A fresh examination of the problem of Marxism and philosophy would also seem to be an important part of this restoration. A negative judgement is clear from the start. The minimization of philosophical problems by most Marxist theoreticians of the Second International was only a *partial expression* of the loss of the practical, revolutionary character of the Marxist movement which found its *general expression* in the simultaneous decay of the living principles of dialectical materialism in the vulgar-marxism of the epigones. We have already mentioned that Marx and Engels themselves always denied that scientific socialism was any longer a philosophy. But it is easy to show irrefutably, by reference to the sources, that what the revolutionary dialecticians Marx and Engels meant by the opposite of philosophy was something very

42. The dialectical interrelationship of Lenin's theory and practice is most clearly shown in a few words from his Afterword to *State and Revolution*, written 30 November 1917 in Petrograd (Lenin, *Collected Works*, vol. 25, p. 492): 'The second part of the book, devoted to the lessons of the Russian Revolutions of 1905 and 1917, will probably have to be put off for a long time. It is more pleasant and more useful *to live through* a revolution than *to write about* it.'

different from what it meant to later vulgar-marxism. Nothing was further from them than the claim to impartial, pure, theoretical study, above class differences, made by Hilferding and most of the other Marxists of the Second International.[43] The scientific socialism of Marx and Engels, correctly understood, stands in far greater contrast to these pure sciences of bourgeois society (economics, history or sociology) than it does to the philosophy in which the revolutionary movement of the Third Estate once found its highest theoretical expression.[44] Consequently, one can only wonder at the insight of more recent Marxists who have been misled by a few of Marx's well-known expressions and by a few of the later Engels, into interpreting the Marxist abolition of philosophy as the replacement of this philosophy by a system of abstract and undialectical positive sciences. The real contradiction between Marx's scientific socialism and all bourgeois philosophy *and sciences* consists entirely in the fact that scientific socialism is the theoretical expression of a revolutionary process, which will end with the total abolition of these bourgeois philosophies and sciences, together with the abolition of the material relations that find their ideological expression in them.[45]

43. Cf. for the moment Marx's comments in his *Poverty of Philosophy* (Moscow, p. 120), on the way in which the theoreticians of the proletariat, the socialists and communists, are related to the different schools of the economists, who are the scientific representatives of the bourgeois class – as well as what he says about the character of scientific socialism, as opposed to doctrinaire and utopian socialism and communism: 'From this moment, science, which is a product of the movement of history, has associated itself consciously with it, has ceased to be doctrinaire and has become revolutionary.'

44. Cf. my *Kernpunkte*, pp. 7ff.

45. It will be proved later that this is really all that Marx and Engels mean by the expression 'positive science'. Meanwhile those Marxists

A re-examination of the problem of Marxism and philosophy is therefore very necessary, even on the theoretical level, in order to restore the correct and full sense of Marx's theory, denatured and banalized by the epigones. However, just as in the case of Marxism and the State, this theoretical task really arises from the needs and pressures of revolutionary practice. In the period of revolutionary transition, after its seizure of power, the proletariat must accomplish definite revolutionary tasks in the ideological field, no less than in the political and economic fields – tasks which constantly interact with each other. The scientific theory of Marxism must become again what it was for the authors of the *Communist Manifesto* – not as a simple *return* but as a *dialectical development*: a theory of social revolution that comprises all areas of society as a totality. Therefore we must solve in a dialectically materialist fashion not only 'the question of the relationship of the State to social revolution and of social revolution to the

---

who hold the view discussed above may see the catastrophic error they have committed, by reading a bourgeois scholar on Marx. *Marx und Hegel* (Jena, 1922), by the Swedish author Sven Helander, is an extremely superficial work and full of elementary mistakes; but it goes much further towards an understanding of the philosophical side of Marxism (what it calls the social-democratic conception of the world) than do other bourgeois critics of Marx, or standard vulgar-marxism. The book gives some convincing evidence (pp. 25ff.) to show that one can only talk of 'scientific socialism' in the sense in which Hegel 'criticizes the critics of society, and advises them to study science and to learn to see the necessity and justice of the State, because this would keep them from critical carping'. This passage is typical of the positive and negative sides of Helander's book. He does not give the source of these statements of Hegel's; in fact they come from the Preface to the *Philosophy of Right*. But Hegel is speaking here not of science, but of philosophy. For Marx, science is important not for the reason that philosophy is important for Hegel, because it reconciles man to reality, but rather because it overthrows this reality (see the passage from *The Poverty of Philosophy* quoted above, note 43).

State' (Lenin), but also the 'question of the relationship of ideology to social revolution and of social revolution to ideology'. To avoid these questions in the period before the proletarian revolution leads to opportunism and creates a crisis within Marxism, just as avoidance of the problem of State and revolution in the Second International led to opportunism and indeed provoked a crisis in the camp of Marxism. To evade a definite stand on these ideological problems of the transition can have disastrous political results in the period after the proletarian seizure of State power, because theoretical vagueness and disarray can seriously impede a prompt and energetic approach to problems that then arise in the ideological field. The major issue of the relation of the proletarian revolution to *ideology* was no less neglected by Social Democrat theoreticians than the political problem of the revolutionary dictatorship of the proletariat. Consequently in this new revolutionary period of struggle it must be posed anew and the correct – dialectical and revolutionary – conception of original Marxism must be restored. This task can only be resolved by first investigating the problem which led Marx and Engels to the question of ideology: how is *philosophy* related to the social revolution of the proletariat and how is the social revolution of the proletariat related to philosophy? An answer to this question is indicated by Marx and Engels themselves and may be deduced from Marx's materialist dialectics. It will lead us on to a larger question: how is Marxist materialism related to *ideology* in general?

What is the relation of the scientific socialism of Marx and Engels to philosophy? 'None,' replies vulgar-marxism. In this perspective it is precisely the new materialist and scientific standpoint of Marxism which has refuted and superseded the old idealist philosophical standpoint. All philosophical ideas and speculations are thereby shown to be unreal – vacuous fantasies which still haunt a few minds as a kind of superstition, which the ruling class has a concrete material interest in preserving. Once capitalism is overthrown the remains of these fantasies will disappear at once.

One has only to reflect on this approach to philosophy in all its shallowness, as we have tried to do, to realize at once that such a solution to the problem of philosophy has nothing in common with the spirit of Marx's modern dialectical materialism. It belongs to the age in which that 'genius of bourgeois stupidity', Jeremy Bentham, explained 'Religion' in his Encyclopedia with the rubric '*vide* superstitious opinions'.[46] It is part of an atmosphere which was created in the seventeenth and eighteenth centuries, and which inspired Eugen Dühring to write that in a future society, constructed according to his plans, there would be no religious cults; for a correctly understood system of sociability would *suppress* all the apparatus needed for spiritual sorcery, and with it all the essential components of these cults.[47] The outlook with which modern or dialectical materialism – the new and *only* scientific view of the world according to Marx and Engels – confronts these questions is in complete contrast to this shallow, rationalist and negative approach to ideological phenomena such as religion and philosophy. To present this contrast in all its bluntness one can say: it is essential for modern dialectical materialism to grasp philosophies and other ideological systems in theory as realities, and to treat them in practice as such. In their early period Marx and Engels began their whole revolutionary activity by struggling against the reality of philosophy; and it will be shown that, although later they

46. Cf. Marx's remarks about Bentham, *Capital*, vol. I, pp. 609–11.

47. Cf. Engels' bitter witticisms on this subject in *Anti-Dühring*, pp. 434ff.

did radically alter their view of how philosophical ideology was related to other forms within ideology as a whole, they always treated ideologies – including philosophy – as concrete realities and not as empty fantasies.

In the 1840s Marx and Engels began the revolutionary struggle – initially on a theoretical and philosophical plane – for the emancipation of the class which stands 'not in partial opposition to the consequences, but in total opposition to the premisses' of existing society as a whole.[48] They were convinced that they were thereby attacking an extremely important part of the existing social order. In the editorial of the *Kölnische Zeitung* in 1842, Marx had already stated that 'philosophy does not stand outside the world, just as the brain does not stand outside man merely because it is not in his stomach'.[49] He repeats this later in the Introduction to the *Critique of Hegel's Philosophy of Right*: 'Previous philosophy itself belongs to this world and is its, albeit idealist, elaboration.'[50] This is the work of which fifteen years later, in the Preface to the *Critique of Political Economy*, Marx said that in it he definitively accomplished the transition to his later materialist position. Precisely when Marx, the dialectician, effected this transition from the idealist to the materialist conception, he made it quite explicit that the practically oriented political party in Germany at the time, which *rejected* all philosophy, was making as big a mistake as the theoretically oriented political party, which *failed to condemn* philosophy as such. The latter believed that it could combat the reality of the German world from a purely philosophical

48. Cf. 'Introduction to the *Critique of Hegel's Philosophy of Right*', in Marx and Engels, *On Religion*, pp. 56–7.

49. 'The Leading Article of no. 179 of the *Kölnische Zeitung*', ibid., p. 30.

50. 'Introduction to the *Critique of Hegel's Philosophy of Right*', ibid., p. 49.

standpoint, that is, with propositions that were derived in one way or another from philosophy (much as Lassalle was later to do by invoking Fichte). It forgot that the philosophical standpoint itself was part of this dominant German world. But the practically oriented political party was basically trapped by the same limitation because it believed that the negation of philosophy 'can be accomplished by turning one's back on philosophy, looking in the opposite direction and mumbling some irritable and banal remarks about it'. It too did not regard 'philosophy as part of German reality'. The theoretically oriented party erroneously believed that 'it could realize philosophy in practice without superseding it in theory'. The practically oriented party made a comparable mistake by trying to supersede philosophy in practice without realizing it in theory – in other words, without grasping it as a reality.[51]

It is clear in what sense Marx (and Engels who underwent an identical development at the same time – as he and Marx often later explained)[52] had now really surpassed the merely philosophical standpoint of his student days; but one can also see how this process itself still had a philosophical character. There are three reasons why we can speak of a surpassal of the philosophical standpoint. First, Marx's theoretical standpoint here is not just partially opposed to the consequences of all existing German philosophy, but is in total opposition to its premisses; (for both Marx and Engels this philosophy was always more than sufficiently represented by Hegel). Second, Marx is opposed not just to philosophy, which is only the head or ideal elaboration of the existing world, but to this world as a totality. Third, and most importantly, this opposition is not just theoretical but is also practical and active. 'The

51. ibid., pp. 48–9.

52. Cf. Marx's remark in the Preface to the *Critique of Political Economy* (1859), *Selected Works*, vol. I, p. 364.

philosophers have only interpreted the world, our task is to change it', announces the last of the *Theses on Feuerbach.* Nevertheless, this general surpassal of the purely philosophical standpoint still incorporates a philosophical character. This becomes clear, once one realizes how little this new proletarian science differs from previous philosophy in its theoretical character, even though Marx substitutes it for bourgeois idealist philosophy as a system radically distinct in its orientation and aims. German idealism had constantly tended, *even on the theoretical level,* to be more than just a theory or philosophy. This is comprehensible in the light of its relation to the revolutionary movement of the bourgeoisie (discussed above), and will be studied further in a later work. This tendency was typical of Hegel's predecessors – Kant, Schelling and especially Fichte. Although Hegel himself to all appearances reversed it, he too in fact allotted philosophy a task that went beyond the realm of theory and became in a certain sense practical. This task was not of course to change the world, as it was for Marx, but rather to reconcile Reason as a self-conscious Spirit with Reason as an actual Reality, by means of concepts and comprehension.[53] German idealism from Kant to Hegel did not cease to be philosophical when it affirmed this universal role (which is anyway what is colloquially thought to be the essence of *any* philosophy). Similarly it is incorrect to say that Marx's materialist theory is no longer philosophical merely because it has an aim that is not simply theoretical but is also a practical and revolutionary goal. On the contrary, the dialectical materialism of Marx and Engels is by its very nature a philosophy through and through, as formulated in the eleventh thesis on Feuerbach and in other

53. See the Preface to the *Philosophy of Right*, p. 12, and also the remarks on Helander, note 45 above.

published and unpublished writings of the period.[54] It is a revolutionary philosophy whose task is to participate in the revolutionary struggles waged in all spheres of society against the whole of the existing order, by fighting in one specific area – philosophy. Eventually, it aims at the concrete abolition of philosophy as part of the abolition of bourgeois social reality as a whole, of which it is an ideal component. In Marx's words: 'Philosophy cannot be abolished without being realized.' Thus just when Marx and Engels were progressing from Hegel's dialectical idealism to dialectical materialism, it is clear that the abolition of philosophy did not mean for them its simple rejection. Even when their later positions are under consideration, it is essential to take it as a constant starting point that Marx and Engels were dialecticians before they were materialists. The sense of their materialism is distorted in a disastrous and irreparable manner if one forgets that

54. Apart from the *Critique of Hegel's Philosophy of Right*, which has been frequently mentioned already, this includes the critique of Bauer's *The Jewish Question* (1843–4), *The Holy Family* and, most important of all, the great settling of their accounts with post-Hegelian philosophy which Marx and Engels carried out together in *The German Ideology* of 1845. The importance of this work for the present discussion is indicated by the remark in the Preface to *The Holy Family*, in which the authors state that their next works will present their own positive conception of, and hence their positive relationship to, 'more recent philosophical and social doctrines'. This text is of the greatest importance for a comprehensive textual study of the problem of Marxism and philosophy, but regrettably it has not yet been published in full. However, even those parts that have already been published (especially *St Max* and *The Leipzig Council*), as well as Gustav Mayer's extremely interesting remarks on the unpublished parts of the manuscript in his biography of Engels, *Friedrich Engels* (German ed. pp. 239–60), enable one to see that it is here that a comprehensive exposition of the dialectical-materialist principle can be found. This cannot be said of the *Communist Manifesto* or of the *Critique of Political Economy*, which present the materialist principle in a largely one-sided way: either stressing its practical and revolutionary side, or its theoretical, economic and historical side. The famous sentences in the Preface to the

Marxist materialism was dialectical from the very beginning. It always remained a historical and dialectical materialism, in contrast to Feuerbach's abstract-scientific materialism and all other abstract materialisms, whether earlier or later, bourgeois or vulgar-marxist. In other words, it was a materialism whose theory comprehended the totality of society and history, and whose practice overthrew it. It was therefore possible for philosophy to become a less central component of the socio-historical process for Marx and Engels, in the course of their development of materialism, than it had seemed at the start; this did in fact occur. But no really dialectical materialist conception of history (certainly not that of Marx and Engels) could cease to regard philosophical ideology, or ideology in general, as a material component of general socio-historical reality – that is, a real part which had to be grasped in materialist theory and overthrown by materialist practice.

Critique of Political Economy on the materialist conception of history are only intended to provide the reader with 'the guiding thread for the study of society', which Marx has used in his analysis of political economy. Hence Marx did *not intend* this passage to express in full *the whole* of his new principle of dialectical materialism. This is often overlooked, although it is perfectly clear from both the content of these remarks, and from their very tone. For example, Marx states that in a period of social revolution men become conscious of the conflict that has broken out and they participate in it; humanity adopts certain tasks only under certain conditions; and the period of revolution itself has a specific consciousness. This makes it clear that there is absolutely no discussion here of the problem of the historical *subject* which accomplishes the real development of society with either a true or a false consciousness. Given all this, if one wants to see the dialectical-materialist principle as a whole, one must complement this description of the materialist conception by those found in the other works of Marx and Engels, especially on the writings of the first period already mentioned (as well as *Capital* and the shorter historical writings of the later period). A preliminary attempt at doing this was made in my little book, published last year (1922), *Kernpunkte der materialistischen Geschichtsauffassung.*

In his *Theses on Feuerbach* Marx contrasts his new materialism not only to philosophical idealism, but just as forcefully to every existing materialism. Similarly, *in all their later writings*, Marx and Engels emphasized the contrast between their dialectical materialism and the normal, abstract and undialectical version of materialism. They were especially conscious that this contrast was of great importance for any theoretical interpretation of so-called mental or ideological realities, and their treatment in practice. Discussing mental representations in general, and the method necessary for a concrete and critical history of religion in particular, Marx states: 'It is in fact much easier to uncover the earthly kernel within nebulous religious ideas, through analysis, than it is to do the opposite, to see how these heavenly forms develop out of actual concrete relations. The latter is the only materialist and therefore scientific method.'[55] A theoretical method which was content

55. *Capital*, vol. I, pp. 372–3n, and the fourth of the eleven *Theses on Feuerbach* which says exactly the same thing. It is easy to see that what Marx here calls the one materialist and therefore scientific method is none other than the method of dialectical materialism, as opposed to the inadequacy of abstract materialism. Cf. Engels' letter to Mehring, 14 July 1893 (*Selected Correspondence*, pp. 540ff.) discussing what is missing from Mehring's use of the materialist method in his *Lessing-Legende* and which 'Marx and I did not generally stress enough in our writings'. 'We all laid, and were bound to lay, the main emphasis on the fact that political, juridical and other ideological notions *are derived* from basic economic facts and that this also applied to actions mediated through these notions. We stressed the content and neglected the form, i.e. the ways and means by which these notions come about.' It will be shown later that this self-criticism Engels makes of his and Marx's writings applies only slightly to the method he and Marx in fact used. The partiality which he criticizes occurs infinitely less in Marx than in Engels himself; but it does not occur in Engels anything like as much as one might expect from his strong criticism of himself. Engels was afraid he had not given enough attention to this formal side and this led him in his later period to make the mistake of sometimes approaching it in an

in good Feuerbachian fashion to reduce all ideological representations to their material and earthly kernel would be abstract and undialectical. A revolutionary practice confined to direct action against the terrestrial kernel of nebulous religious ideas, and unconcerned with overthrowing and superseding these ideologies themselves, would be no less so. When vulgar-marxism adopts this abstract and negative attitude to the reality of ideologies, it makes exactly the same mistake as those proletarian theoreticians, past and present, who use the Marxist thesis of the economic determination of legal relations, state forms and political action, to argue that the proletariat can and should confine itself to direct economic action alone.[56] It is well known that Marx strongly attacked

---

incorrect and undialectical way. This applies to all the passages in *Anti-Dühring* and *Ludwig Feuerbach*, and especially in Engels's later letters, which concern the 'area to which the materialist conception of history can validly be applied'; these letters were collected by Bernstein in *Dokumente des Sozialismus*, II, pp. 65ff. (*Selected Correspondence*, letters 214, 215, 232, 234, etc.). In them Engels tends to make the very mistake that Hegel describes in paragraph 156 of his *Encyclopaedia* (*The Logic of Hegel*, Wallace translation, 1864, p. 242) as a 'really unintelligent procedure'. In Hegel's terms, he retreats from the height of the concept to its threshold, to the categories of reacting and mutual interaction, etc.

56. A highly typical example of this outmoded view can be found in Proudhon's famous letter of May 1846 in which he explained to Marx how he saw the problem at that time (*Nachlass*, vol. II, p. 336): 'To give back to society by means of an economic combination of wealth that which has been taken out of society by another combination; in other words, to convert the theory of property into political economy, to turn it against property and thereby to achieve what you German socialists call a community of goods.' Marx, on the other hand, although he had certainly not yet attained his mature dialectical-materialist position, had nevertheless come to see quite clearly the dialectical relationship whereby economic questions must also be posed and resolved on the political plane theoretically and practically. Cf. Marx's letter to Ruge, of September 1843, where he talks of those 'crass socialists' who

tendencies of this kind in his polemics against Proudhon and others. In different phases of his life, wherever he came across views like this, which still survive in contemporary syndicalism, Marx always emphasized that this 'transcendental underestimation' of the State and political action was completely unmaterialist. It was therefore theoretically inadequate and practically dangerous.[57]

This dialectical conception of the relationship of economics to politics became such an unalterable part of Marxist theory that even the vulgar-marxists of the Second International were unable to deny that the problem of the revolutionary transition existed, at least *in theory*, although they ignored the problem *in practice*. No orthodox Marxist could even in principle have claimed that a theoretical and practical concern with politics was unnecessary for Marxism. This was left to the syndicalists, some of whom invoke Marx, but none of whom have ever claimed to be orthodox Marxists. However, many good Marxists did adopt a theoretical and practical position on the reality of ideology which was identical to that of the syndicalists. These materialists are with Marx in condemning the syndicalist refusal of political action and in declaring that the social movement must include the political movement. They often argue against anarchists that even after the victorious proletarian revolution, and in spite of all the changes undergone by the bourgeois State, politics will long continue to be a reality. Yet these very people fall straight into the anarcho-syndicalist 'transcendental underestimation' of ideology when

---

regard political questions like the difference between the estate system and the representative system as 'beneath contempt'. Marx replies with the dialectical consideration that 'this question expresses in political form the difference between the domination of men and the domination of private property' (*Nachlass*, I, p. 382).

57. Cf. in particular the last pages of the *The Poverty of Philosophy*.

they are told that *intellectual* struggle in the ideological field cannot be replaced or eliminated by the social movement of the proletariat alone, or by its social and political movements combined. Even today most Marxist theoreticians conceive of the efficacy of so-called intellectual phenomena in a purely negative, abstract and undialectical sense, when they should analyse this domain of social reality with the materialist and scientific method moulded by Marx and Engels. Intellectual life should be conceived in union with social and political life, and social being and becoming (in the widest sense, as economics, politics or law) should be studied in union with social consciousness in its many different manifestations, as a real yet also ideal (or 'ideological') component of the historical process in general. Instead, all consciousness is approached with totally abstract and basically metaphysical dualism, and declared to be a reflection of the one really concrete and material developmental process, on which it is completely dependent (even if relatively independent, still dependent in the last instance).[58]

Given this situation, any theoretical attempt to restore what Marx regarded as the only scientific, dialectical materialist conception and treatment of *ideological* realities, inevitably encounters even greater theoretical obstacles than an attempt to restore the correct Marxist theory of the State. The distortion of Marxism by the epigones in the question of the *State* and *politics* merely consisted in the fact that the most prominent theoreticians of the Second International never dealt concretely enough with the most vital political problems of the revolutionary transition. However, they at least agreed in abstract, and emphasized strongly in their long struggles against anarchists and syndicalists that, for materialism, not

58. See note 55 for the extent to which the later Engels made concessions to this in the end.

only the economic structure of society, which underlay all other socio-historical phenomena, but also the juridical and political superstructure of Law and the State were *realities.* Consequently, they could not be ignored or dismissed in an anarcho-syndicalist fashion: they had to be overthrown in reality by a political revolution. In spite of this, many vulgar-marxists to this day have never, even in theory, admitted that intellectual life and forms of social consciousness are comparable realities. Quoting certain statements by Marx and especially Engels they simply explain away the *intellectual (ideological) structures of society* as a mere *pseudo-reality* which only exists in the minds of ideologues – as error, imagination and illusion, devoid of a genuine object.[59] At any rate, this is supposed to be true for all the so-called 'higher' ideologies. For this conception, political and legal representatives may have an ideological and unreal character, but they are at least related to something real – the institutions of Law and the State, which comprise the superstructure of the society in question. On the other hand, the 'higher' ideological representations (men's religions, aesthetic and philosophical conceptions) correspond to no real object. This can be formulated concisely, with only a slight caricature, by saying that for vulgar-marxism there are *three degrees of reality*: (1) the economy, which in the last instance is the only objective and totally non-ideological reality; (2) Law and the State, which are already somewhat less real because clad in ideology, and (3) pure ideology which is objectless and totally unreal ('pure rubbish').

59. Later in life Engels did once regrettably say of such 'realms of ideology that float still higher in the air' as religion of philosophy, that they contained a pre-historic element of 'primitive stupidity' (letter to Conrad Schmidt, 27 October 1890, *Selected Correspondence*, p. 505). In *Theories on Surplus Value* Marx also talks specifically of philosophy in a similar, *apparently* quite negative tone.

To restore a genuine dialectically materialist conception of intellectual reality, it is first necessary to make a few mainly terminological points. The key problem to settle here is how in general to approach the relationship of consciousness to its object. Terminologically, it must be said that it never occurred to Marx and Engels to describe social consciousness and intellectual life merely as ideology. Ideology is only a false consciousness, in particular one that mistakenly attributes an autonomous character to a partial phenomena of social life. Legal and political representations which conceive Law and the State to be independent forces above society are cases in point.[60] In the passage where Marx is most precise about his terminology,[61] he says explicitly that within the complex of material relations that Hegel called civil society, the social relations of production – the economic structure of society – forms the real foundation on which arise juridical and political superstructures and to which determinate forms of social consciousness correspond. In particular, these forms of social consciousness, which are no less real than Law and the State, include commodity fetishism, the concept of value, and other economic representations derived from them. Marx and Engels analysed these in their critique of political economy. What is strikingly characteristic of their treatment is that they

60. Cf. in particular Engels' remarks on the State in *Ludwig Feuerbach* (*Selected Works*, vol. 2, p. 396).

61. Cf. the Preface to the *Critique of Political Economy* (*Selected Works*, vol. II, p. 363). One can find a meticulous collection of all the philological and methodological material on this question in the work of a bourgeois scholar on Marx, Hammacher's *Das philosophisch-ökonomische System des Marxismus* (1909), pp. 190–206. Hammacher distinguishes himself from other bourgeois critics of Marx by the fact that, in attempting to solve this problem, he at least draws on all the textual material, while others, such as Tönnies and Barth, had based their interpretations on isolated phrases and passages of Marx.

never refer to this basic economic ideology of bourgeois society as an ideology. In their terminology only the legal, political, religious, aesthetic or philosophical forms of consciousness are ideological. Even these need not be so in all situations, but become so only under specific conditions which have already been stated. The special position now allotted to forms of economic consciousness marks the new conception of philosophy which distinguishes the fully matured dialectical materialism of the later period from its undeveloped earlier version. The theoretical and practical criticisms of philosophy is henceforward relegated to the second, third, fourth or even last but one place in their critique of society. The 'critical philosophy' which the Marx of the *Deutsch-Französische Jahrbücher* saw as his essential task[62] became a more radical critique of society, which went to the roots of it[63] through a critique of political economy. Marx once said that a critic could '*start from any form of philosophical and practical consciousness* and develop from the specific forms of existent reality, its true reality and final end'.[64] But he later became aware that no juridical relations, constitutional structures or forms of social consciousness can be understood in themselves or even in Hegelian or post-Hegelian terms of the general development of the human Spirit. For they are *rooted* in the material conditions of life that form 'the material basis and skeleton' of social organization as a whole.[65] A radical critique of bourgeois society can no longer start from 'any' form

62. Marx to Ruge, September 1843, *Nachlass*, vol. 1, p. 383.

63. This is how Marx defines the word 'radical' in his 'Introduction to the *Critique of Hegel's Philosophy of Right*', *On Religion*, p. 50.

64. Marx to Ruge, September 1843, loc. cit., p. 381.

65. Introduction to the *Critique of Political Economy* (Chicago, 1904) p. 310; see also the Preface in ibid., and *Selected Works*, vol. I.

of theoretical or practical consciousness whatever, as Marx thought as late as 1843.[66] It must start from the particular forms of consciousness which have found their scientific expression in the political economy of bourgeois society. Consequently the critique of political economy is theoretically and practically the first priority. Yet even this deeper and more radical version of Marx's revolutionary critique of society never ceases to be a critique of the *whole* of bourgeois society and so of *all* its forms of consciousness. It may seem as if Marx and Engels were later to criticize philosophy only in an

66. This was not a completely accurate account of Marx's real position, even in 1843. The words in the text come from Marx's letter to Ruge of September 1843, but a few lines later he says that the issues which preoccupy the representatives of the socialist principle concern the reality of true human nature. However, they also need to criticize the other side of this nature – man's theoretical existence in religion, science, etc. Marx's development can be summarized as follows. First, he criticized religion philosophically. Then he criticized religion and philosophy politically. Finally, he criticized religion, philosophy, politics and all other ideologies economically. The milestones on this road are: 1. The remarks in the preface to his philosophical thesis (a philosophical critique of religion). 2. The remarks on Feuerbach in his letter to Ruge, dated 13 March 1843: 'There is only one thing wrong with Feuerbach's aphorisms. They lay too much stress on nature and not enough on politics. That is the one link by which contemporary philosophy can become true.' There is also the famous remark in the September 1843 letter to Ruge mentioned above, where he says that philosophy has 'secularized' itself and thereby 'philosophical consciousness itself has been drawn into the agony of struggle not only externally but also internally'. 3. The statement in the 'Introduction to the *Critique of Hegel's Philosophy of Right*' that 'the way industry and the world of wealth as a whole relate to the world of politics', is 'a major issue of modern times'. This problem has been posed by 'modern socio-political reality itself', but it stands outside the *status quo* of German legal and state philosophy, and even of its 'final, richest and most consistent' form in Hegel (*On Religion*, pp. 13–15; *Dokumente des Sozialismus*, I, pp. 396–7; *Nachlass*, I, p. 380; 'Introduction to the *Critique of Hegel's Philosophy of Right*', *On Religion*, pp. 47ff.).

occasional and haphazard manner. In fact, far from neglecting the subject, they actually developed their critique of it in a more profound and radical direction. For proof, it is only necessary to re-establish the full revolutionary meaning of Marx's critique of political economy, as against certain mistaken ideas about it which are common today. This may also serve to clarify both its place in the whole system of Marx's critique of society, and its relation to his critique of ideologies like philosophy.

It is generally accepted that the critique of political economy – the most important theoretical and practical component of the Marxist theory of society – includes not only a critique of the material relations of production of the capitalist epoch but also of its specific forms of social consciousness. Even the pure and impartial 'scientific science' of vulgar-marxism acknowledges this. Hilferding admits that scientific knowledge of the economic laws of a society is also a 'scientific politics' in so far as it shows 'the determinant factors which define the *will of the classes* in this society'. Despite this relation of economics to politics, however, in the totally abstract and undialectical conception of vulgar-marxism, the 'critique of political economy' has a purely theoretical role as a 'science'. Its function is to criticize the errors of bourgeois economics, classical or vulgar. By contrast, a proletarian political party uses the results of critical and scientific investigation for its practical ends – ultimately the overthrow of the real economic structure of capitalist society and of its relations of production. (On occasion, the results of this Marxism can also be used against the proletarian party itself, as by Simkhovitch or Paul Lensch.)

The major weakness of vulgar socialism is that, in Marxist terms, it clings quite 'unscientifically' to a naïve realism – in which both so-called common sense, which is the 'worst metaphysician', and the normal positivist science of bourgeois society, draw a sharp line of division between consciousness and its object. Neither are aware that this distinction had ceased to be completely valid even for the transcendental perspective of critical philosophy,[67] and has been completely superseded in dialectical philosophy.[68] At best, they imagine

67. Lask's remarks on this are particularly instructive (in the second section of his 'Philosophy of Right' in *Festgabe für Kuno Fischer*, II, pp. 28ff.).

68. An excellent illustration of this is Book II, chapter 3, of *On War* (Penguin Classics, pp. 201–03, 'Art or Science of War') by General von Clausewitz, a philosopher of war who was deeply influenced by the spirit and method of idealist philosophy. Clausewitz asks whether one should speak of the art of war or rather of the science of war, and he comes to the conclusion that 'it is more fitting to say the art of war than the science of war'. But this does not satisfy him. He goes on to say that, on closer inspection, war 'is neither an art nor a science in the real sense of the word' and neither is it in its modern form a 'handicraft' (as it used to be at the time of the *condottieri*). In fact war is far more 'part of human intercourse'. 'We say therefore that war belongs not to the realm of the arts and sciences, but to the realm of social life. It is a conflict of great interests which is settled by blood and only in that respect is it different from others. It would be better, instead of comparing it with any art, to liken it to trade, which is also a conflict of human interests and activities; and it is much more like politics, which in its turn may be looked upon as a kind of trade on a great scale. Besides, politics is the womb in which war is developed, in which its outlines lie hidden in a rudimentary state, like the qualities of living creatures in their germs.' Some modern positivist thinkers who are influenced by fixed metaphysical categories might well criticize this theory on the grounds that Clausewitz has confused the object of the science of war with the science itself. In fact, Clausewitz knew perfectly well what is usually and undialectically meant by 'science'. He expressly says that there cannot be a science 'in the real sense of the word' which has as its object what is normally called either the art of war or the science of war. This is because it does not deal with 'inanimate matter' as in the mechanical arts (and sciences), or with a 'living, but passive and submissive object' as in the ideal arts (and sciences): it deals with a 'living and *reacting*' object. Like every other non-transcendent object, it can be 'illuminated by an inquiring mind and its inner structure more or less clarified', and

that something like this might be true of Hegel's idealist dialectic. It is precisely this, they think, that constitutes the 'mystification' which the dialectic, according to Marx, 'suffered at Hegel's hands'. It follows therefore for them that this mystification must be completely eliminated from the rational form of the dialectic: the materialist dialectic of Marx. In fact, we shall show, Marx and Engels were very far from having any such dualistic metaphysical conception of the relationship of consciousness to reality – not only in their first (philosophical) period but also in their second (positive-scientific) period. It never occurred to them that they could be misunderstood in this dangerous way. Precisely because of this, they sometimes did provide considerable pretexts for such misunderstandings in certain of their formulations (although these can easily be corrected by a hundred times as many other formulations). For the *coincidence of consciousness and reality* characterizes every dialectic, including Marx's dialectical materialism. Its consequence is that the material relations of production of the capitalist epoch only are what

---

'that alone is sufficient to justify the idea of a theory' (ibid., p. 203). Clausewitz's concept of theory is so like the concept of science in the scientific socialism of Marx and Engels that there is no need to say more about it. This is not at all surprising because both have the same source: Hegel's dialectical conception of philosophy and science. Moreover, the comments of Clausewitz's epigones on this aspect of their master's theory are very strikingly similar, in tone and content, to corresponding remarks by some modern scientific Marxists about Marx's theory. Here is a passage from Schlieffen's preface (p. 4) to his edition of Clausewitz: 'Clausewitz did not dispute that a sound theory is in itself valuable, but his book *On War* is permeated by an attempt to bring theory into harmony with the real world. This partly explains the predominance of a philosophizing way of approaching things which does not always appeal to a modern reader.' As one can see, it was not just Marxism that was vulgarized in the second half of the nineteenth century.

they are in combination with the forms in which they are reflected in the pre-scientific and bourgeois-scientific consciousness of the period; and they could not subsist in reality without these forms of consciousness. Setting aside any philosophical considerations, it is therefore clear that *without this coincidence of consciousness and reality, a critique of political economy could never have become the major component of a theory of social revolution.* The converse follows. Those Marxist theoreticians for whom Marxism was no longer essentially a theory of social revolution could see no need for this dialectical conception of the coincidence of reality and consciousness: it was bound to appear to them as theoretically false and unscientific.[69]

In the different periods of their revolutionary activity, Marx and Engels speak of the relationship of consciousness to reality at the economic level, or the higher levels of politics and law, or on the highest levels of art, religion and philosophy. It is always necessary to ask in what direction these remarks are aimed (they are nearly always, above all in the late period, only remarks!). For their import is very different,

69. This relationship between a non-revolutionary spirit and a complete misinterpretation of the dialectical aspect of Marx's critique of political economy is particularly obvious in Eduard Bernstein. He concludes his exposition of different aspects of the theory of value (*Dokumente des Sozialismus*, 1905, p. 559) with a remark that contrasts curiously with the real meaning of Marx's theory of value: 'Today we [*sic*] investigate the laws of price formation in a more direct way than by going through the maze of that metaphysical object called "value".' Similarly, socialist idealists of the back-to-Kant variety and other tendencies separate fact from value. Cf. Helander's naïve criticism in *Marx und Hegel*, p. 26: 'Most men naturally tend to think in Kantian terms, i.e. to acknowledge a difference between "is" and "ought".' See also Marx's remarks about John Locke in *Critique of Political Economy*, p. 93, where he says that this penetrating bourgeois philosopher 'went so far as to prove in his own work that bourgeois reason is normal human reason'.

depending on whether they are aimed at Hegel's idealist and speculative method or at 'the ordinary method, essentially Wolff's metaphysical method, which has become fashionable once again'. After Feuerbach had 'dispatched speculative concepts', the latter re-emerged in the new natural-scientific materialism of Büchner, Vogt and Moleschott and 'even bourgeois economists wrote large rambling books' inspired by it.[70] From the outset, Marx and Engels had to clarify their position only with regard to the first, Hegelian method. They never doubted that they had issued from it. Their only problem was how to change the Hegelian dialectic from a method proper to a superficially idealist, but secretly materialist conception of the world, into the guiding principle of an explicitly materialist view of history and society.[71] Hegel had already taught that a philosophico-scientific method was not a mere form of thought which could be applied indiscriminately to any content. It was rather 'the structure of the whole presented in its pure essence'. Marx made the same point in an early writing: 'Form has no value if it is not the form of

70. The best account of the whole methodological situation is found in the second of two articles Engels wrote on Marx's *Critique of Political Economy*, which were published in August 1859 in *Das Volk*, a German magazine issued in London (Marx and Engels, *Selected Works*, vol. I, pp. 366ff.). The phrases quoted here, and many other similar ones, are found on pp. 371ff. ('It seemed as if the reign of the old metaphysics with its fixed categories had begun anew in science', at a 'time when the positive content of science once again prevailed over its formal aspect'; when natural sciences 'became fashionable' 'there was a recrudescence of the old metaphysical manner of thinking, including the extreme platitudes of Wolff'; 'they totally reproduced the narrow-minded philistine way of thinking of the pre-Kantian period'; 'the obstinate cart-horse of bourgeois common sense', etc., etc.)

71. For the way in which the relationship between the Hegelian and Marxist *conceptions of history* differed from the relationship between the Hegelian and Marxist *logical methods*, see Engels, ibid., p. 373.

its content.'[72] As Marx and Engels said, it then became a – logical and methodological – question of 'stripping the dialectical method of its idealist shell and presenting it in the simple form in which it becomes the only correct form of intellectual development'.[73] Marx and Engels were confronted with the abstract speculative form in which Hegel bequeathed the dialectical method and which the different Hegelian schools had developed in an even more abstract and formal way. They therefore made vigorous counter-statements, such as: all thought is nothing but the 'transformation of perceptions and representations into concepts'; even the most general categories of thought are only 'abstract, unilateral relations of a living totality that is already given'; an object which thought comprehends as real 'remains as before, independent and external to the mind'.[74] Nevertheless, all their lives they rejected the undialectical approach which counterposes the

72. Cf. *Nachlass*, I, p. 319, 'Proceedings of the Sixth Rhine Parliament. Debates on the Law to Prevent the Theft of Wood'. The phrase from Hegel (from the *Phenomenology of the Spirit*) is quoted at greater length in my *Kernpunkte*, pp. 38ff. The inability to comprehend this relationship of identity between form and content distinguishes the transcendental from the dialectical standpoint (whether idealist or materialist). The former regards content as empirical and historical, form as generally valid and necessary; the latter sees form as also subject to empirical and historical transcience and hence to the 'agony of the struggle'. This passage clearly illustrates how pure democracy and pure transcendental philosophy are related.

73. Engels, op. cit., p. 373; he adds that the working out of this *method* in Marx's *Critique of Political Economy* is an achievement 'of hardly less importance than the *basic materialist conception*'. Cf. also Marx's own well-known statements in the afterword to the second edition of *Capital* (1873).

74. All these expressions are from the posthumously published Introduction to the *Critique of Political Economy*, which is the richest source for studying the real methodological position of Marx and Engels.

thought, observation, perception and comprehension of an immediately given reality *to* this reality, as if the former were themselves also immediately given independent essences. This is best shown by a sentence from Engels' attack on Dühring, which is doubly conclusive because it is widely believed that the later Engels degenerated into a thoroughly naturalistic-materialist view of the world by contrast to Marx, his more philosophically literate companion. It is precisely in one of his last writings that Engels, in the same breath as he describes thought and consciousness as products of the human brain and man himself as a product of nature, also unambiguously protests against the wholly 'naturalistic' outlook which accepts consciousness and thought 'as something given, something straightforwardly opposed to Being and to Nature'.[75] The method of Marx and Engels is not that of an abstract materialism, but of a dialectical materialism: it is therefore the only scientific method. For Marxism, pre-scientific, extra-scientific and scientific consciousness[76] no longer exist over and against

75. Engels, *Anti-Dühring* (Moscow), p. 55. A more thorough analysis of these statements of Engels in his later writings shows that he merely accentuated a tendency that was already present in Marx. Engels took all socio-historic phenomena (including socio-historic forms of consciousness) which were determined 'in the last instance' by the economy, and added to them yet another, even more final 'determination by nature'. This last twist of Engels develops and sustains historical materialism; but, as the quotation in the text shows quite clearly, it in no way alters the dialectical conception of the relationship between consciousness and reality.

76. The term 'pre-scientific conceptualization' is known to have been coined by the Kantian Rickert. The notion is naturally bound to turn up where either a transcendental or dialectical approach is applied to the social sciences (e.g. in Dilthey). Marx draws a sharp and precise distinction between 'intellectual appropriation of the world by the thinking mind' and 'the appropriation of the world by art, religion and the practical spirit' (*Critique of Political Economy*).

the natural and (above all) social-historical world. They exist within this world as a real and objective component of it, if also an 'ideal' one. This is the first specific difference between the materialist dialectic of Marx and Engels, and Hegel's idealist dialectic. Hegel said that the theoretical consciousness of an individual could not 'leap over' his own epoch, the world of his time. Nevertheless he inserted the world into philosophy far more than he did philosophy into the world. This first difference between the Hegelian and Marxist dialectic is very closely related to a second one. As early as 1844 Marx wrote in *The Holy Family*: 'Communist workers well know that property, capital, money, wage-labour and suchlike, far from being idealist fantasies are highly practical and objective products of their own alienation; they must be transcended in a practical and objective way so that man can become man, not only in thought and in consciousness, but in his (social) Being and in his life.' This passage states with full materialist clarity that, given the unbreakable interconnection of all real phenomena in bourgeois society as a whole, its forms of consciousness cannot be abolished through thought alone. These forms can only be abolished in thought and consciousness by a simultaneous *practico-objective overthrow* of the material relations of production themselves, which have hitherto been comprehended through these forms. This is also true of the highest forms of social consciousness, such as religion, and of medium levels of social being and consciousness, such as the family.[77] This consequence of the new materialism is implied in the *Critique of Hegel's Philosophy of Right*, and is explicitly and comprehensively developed in

77. For the consequences of the new materialist standpoint for religion and the family, see the fourth Thesis on Feuerbach, where they are first developed, and various parts of *Capital.*

the *Theses on Feuerbach* which Marx wrote in 1845 to clarify his own ideas. 'The question of whether objective truth corresponds to human thought is not a theoretical question but a practical one. Man must prove the truth – that is, the reality, the power, and the immanence of his thought, in practice. The dispute about the reality or unreality of thought – thought isolated from practice – is purely scholastic.' It would be a dangerous misunderstanding to think that this means that criticism in practice merely replaces criticism in theory. Such an idea merely replaces the philosophical abstraction of pure theory with an opposite anti-philosophical abstraction of an equally pure practice. It is not in 'human practice' alone, but only 'in human practice and in the comprehension of this practice' that Marx as a dialectical materialist locates the rational solution of all mysteries that 'lure theory into mysticism'. The translation of the dialectics from its mystification by Hegel to the 'rational form' of Marx's materialist dialectic essentially means that it has become the guiding principle of a single theoretical-practical and critical-revolutionary activity. It is a 'method that is by its very nature critical and revolutionary'.[78] Even in Hegel 'the theoretical was essentially contained in the practical'. 'One must not imagine that man thinks on the one hand and wills on the other, that he has Thought in one pocket and Will in another; this would be a vacuous notion'. For Hegel, the practical task of the Concept in its 'thinking activity' (in other words, philosophy) does not lie in the domain of ordinary 'practical human and sensuous activity' (Marx). It is rather 'to grasp what is, for that which is, is Reason'.[79] By contrast, Marx concludes the self-clarifica-

78. Cf. the often-quoted sentences at the end of the postscript to the second edition of *Capital* (1873).

79. Cf. the supplementary passage in section 4 and the last paragraphs of the Preface to the *Philosophy of Right*.

tion of his own dialectical method with the eleventh *Thesis on Feuerbach*: 'The philosophers have only *interpreted* the world, it is now a question of *changing* it.' This does not mean, as the epigones imagine, that all philosophy is shown to be mere fantasy. It only expresses a categorical rejection of all theory, philosophical or scientific, that is not *at the same time* practice – real, terrestrial, immanent, human and sensuous practice, and not the speculative activity of the philosophical idea that basically does nothing but comprehend itself. Theoretical criticism and practical overthrow are here inseparable activities, not in any abstract sense but as a concrete and real alteration of the concrete and real world of bourgeois society. Such is the most precise expression of the new materialist principle of the scientific socialism of Marx and Engels.

We have now shown the real consequences of the dialectical materialist principle for a Marxist conception of the relationship of consciousness to reality. By the same token, we have shown the error of all abstract and undialectical conceptions found among various kinds of vulgar-marxists in their theoretical and practical attitudes to so-called intellectual reality. Marx's dictum is true not just of forms of economic consciousness in the narrower sense, but *all* forms of social consciousness: they are not mere chimeras, but 'highly objective and highly practical' social realities and consequently 'must be abolished in a practical and objective manner'. The naïvely metaphysical standpoint of sound bourgeois common sense considers thought independent of being and defines truth as the correspondence of thought to an object that is external to it and 'mirrored' by it. It is only this outlook that can sustain the view that all forms of economic consciousness (the economic conceptions of a pre-scientific and unscientific consciousness, as well as scientific economics itself) have an objective meaning because they correspond to a reality (the material relations of production which they comprehend) – whereas all higher forms of representation are merely objectless fantasies which will automatically dissolve into their essential nullity after the overthrow of the economic structure of society, and the abolition of its juridical and political superstructure. Economic ideas themselves only *appear* to be related to the material relations of production of bourgeois society in the way an image is related to the object it reflects. In fact they are related to them in the way that a specific, particularly defined part of a whole is related to the other parts of this whole. Bourgeois economics belongs with the material relations of production to bourgeois society as a totality. This totality also contains political and legal representations and their apparent objects, which bourgeois politicians and jurists – the 'ideologues of private property' (Marx) – treat in an ideologically inverted manner as autonomous essences. Finally, it also includes the higher ideologies of the art, religion and philosophy of bourgeois society. If it seems that there are no objects which these representations can reflect, correctly or incorrectly, this is because economic, political or legal representations do not have particular objects which exist independently either, isolated from the other phenomena of bourgeois society. To counterpose such objects to these representations is an abstract and ideological bourgeois procedure. They merely express bourgeois society as a totality in a particular way, just as do art, religion and philosophy. Their ensemble forms the *spiritual structure* of bourgeois society, which corresponds to its economic structure, just as its legal and political superstructure corresponds to this same basis. All these forms must be subjected to the revolutionary social criticism of scientific socialism, which embraces the whole of social reality. They must be criticized in theory and overthrown in practice, together with the economic, legal and political structures of society and at the same time as them.[80] Just as political action is not rendered unnecessary by the economic action of a revolutionary class, so intellectual action is not rendered unnecessary by either political or economic action. On the contrary it must be carried through to the end in theory and practice, as revolutionary scientific criticism and agitational work before the seizure of state power by the working class, and as scientific organization and ideological dictatorship after the seizure of state power. If this is valid for intellectual action against the forms of consciousness which define bourgeois society in general, it is especially true of philosophical action. Bourgeois consciousness necessarily sees itself as apart from the world and independent of it, as pure critical philosophy and impartial science, just as the bourgeois State and bourgeois Law appear to be above society. This consciousness must be philosophically fought by the revolutionary materialistic dialectic, which is the philosophy of the working class. This struggle will only end when the whole of existing society and its economic basis have been totally overthrown in practice, and this consciousness has been totally surpassed and abolished in theory. 'Philosophy cannot be abolished without being realized.'

80. Cf. especially Lenin's statements in his text 'On the Significance of Militant Materialism', *Collected Works*, vol. 33.

The Present State of the Problem of 'Marxism and Philosophy' –An Anti-Critique [1930]

I

*Habent sua fata libelli**. In 1923 there appeared a work on a 'problem of the greatest theoretical and practical importance: the relationship between Marxism and philosophy'. It had a rigorously scientific character, but did not deny that the problem was practically related to the struggles of our age, which were then raging at their fiercest. It was prepared to receive a biased and negative theoretical reception from the tendency which it had attacked in practice. It might, on the other hand, have expected to get a fair and even friendly reception from the tendency whose practical orientation it had represented in theory, and with the tools of theory. The opposite occurred. The evaluation of *Marxism and Philosophy* by *bourgeois* philosophy and science evaded its practical premisses and consequences, and interpreted its theoretical theses in a unilateral manner. Its representatives were therefore able to adopt a positive attitude towards the theoretical content of a work

* To each text its own fate.

they had travestied. They did not provide a concrete presentation and criticism of the real theoretical and practical conclusion which all the analyses of the book served to establish and develop. Instead they unilaterally selected what, from the bourgeois point of view, was supposed to be the 'good' side of the work – its acknowledgement of intellectual realities. They ignored what was indeed the 'bad' side for the bourgeoisie – its call for the total destruction and abolition of these intellectual realities and their material basis: these goals were to be accomplished by a revolutionary class engaged in material and intellectual, practical and theoretical action. Bourgeois critics were thus able to hail a dissociated conclusion of the book as a scientific advance.[1] On the other hand, the authoritative members of the two dominant tendencies of contemporary official 'Marxism' sensed at once, with an unerring instinct, that this unassuming little book contained a heretical rejection of certain dogmas. Despite all their apparent disagreements, the two confessions of the old Marxist orthodox church still held these in common. They were therefore quick to denounce the book before their assembled Councils

1. See, for example, *Politische Literaturberichte der deutschen Hochschule für Politik*, vol. I, no. 2: 'What appears especially noteworthy is the opposition to the vulgar-marxist view that the intellectual (ideological) structure of society is a pseudo-reality. The basic principles of Marxist thought make it quite clear that this structure is of great significance for reality.' Or the conclusions of László Radványi's thorough and penetrating review in *Archiv für Sozialwissenschaften*, LII, 2, pp. 527ff.; 'Even someone who does not share the author's basic convictions must realize from this book that genuine Marxism is not a pan-economism. It does *not* consider the economic structure to be the only realm that is fully real. It recognizes the intellectual sphere to be completely real and to be a constitutive part of the totality of social life' (ibid., p. 535).

for containing views that were a *deviation from accepted doctrine.*[2]

At both Party Congresses in 1924 the relevant ideological authorities reacted by condemning *Marxism and Philosophy* as heretical. What is at once most striking about the critical arguments on which they based this condemnation is the *complete identity of their content* – a somewhat unexpected one for tendencies whose theory and practice diverge in all other respects. The Social Democrat Wels condemned the views of 'Professor Korsch' as a 'Communist' heresy, and the Communist Zinoviev condemned them as a 'Revisionist' heresy. The difference, however, was merely terminological. In point of fact there is nothing new in the arguments directly or indirectly advanced against my views by Bammel and Luppol, Bukharin and Deborin, Béla Kun and Rudas, Thalheimer and Duncker, or other *critics belonging to the communist movement.* (Their attacks are connected with the recent inquisition against George Lukács which I will discuss later.) They have merely repeated and developed ancient arguments of that leading representative of the other camp of official Marxism – Karl Kautsky, *theoretician of the Social Democratic Party.* Kautsky wrote a detailed review of my book in the theoretical journal of German Social Democracy.[3] He was under the

2. Compare the opening speech of party chairman Wels at the 1924 Congress of the Social Democratic Party (reprinted in the official organ of the German Social Democratic Party, *Vorwärts*, 12, June 1924) and the opening speech of the chairman of the Communist International, Zinoviev, at the Fifth World Congress of the Communist International which was taking place at the same time (*Fifth Congress of the Communist International*, published by the Communist Party of Great Britain, p. 17).

3. See *Die Gesellschaft*, I, 3, June 1924, pp. 306ff. The same stereotyped arguments recur in all Communist Party critics, and they can all be found in the critical introduction by the editor, G. Bammel, to a Russian translation of *Marxism and Philosophy* which was issued in

illusion that in attacking my work he was attacking 'all the theoreticians of Communism'. The real dividing line in this debate, however, is quite different. *A fundamental debate on the general state of modern Marxism* has now begun, and there are many indications that despite secondary, transient or trivial conflicts, the real division on all major and decisive questions is between the old Marxist orthodoxy of Kautsky allied to the new Russian or 'Leninist' orthodoxy on the one side, and all critical and progressive theoretical tendencies in the proletarian movement today on the other side.

This general situation of contemporary Marxist theory explains why the great majority of my critics were far less concerned with the *more limited set of questions* defined by the title 'Marxism and Philosophy', than with two other problems which the book did not treat thoroughly but only touched upon. The first is the *conception of Marxism itself* which lies behind all the propositions in my text. The second is the more general problem of the Marxist concept of *ideology*, or of the relationship between *consciousness* and *being*, onto which the specific problem of the relationship between Marxism and philosophy eventually debouched. On this latter point the theses I put forward in 'Marxism and Philosophy' agree in many ways with the propositions, founded on a broader philosophical basis, to be found in the dialectical studies of George Lukács, which appeared about the same time under the title *History and Class Consciousness*. In a 'Postscript' to my work I stated I was fundamentally in agreement with Lukács and postponed any discussion of the specific differences of method and content that remained between us. This

---

1924 by the 'October of the Spirit' publishing house, Moscow. (Another translation without any commentary was issued in 1924 just before this, by 'Kniga', Leningrad and Moscow.)

was then quite incorrectly taken – especially by Communist critics – as an avowal of complete accord between us. In fact, I myself was not sufficiently aware at the time of the extent to which Lukács and I, despite our many theoretical similarities, did in fact diverge in more than just a few 'detailed' points. This is one reason – there are others which this is not the place to discuss – why I did not then respond to the insistent demand of my Communist assailants to 'differentiate' my views from those of Lukács. I preferred to allow these critics to go on indiscriminately assimilating the 'deviations' of Lukács and myself from the one 'Marxist-Leninist' doctrine which alone brings salvation. Today, in this second unaltered edition, I cannot again state that I am in basic agreement with Lukács's views, as I once did. The other reasons which previously restrained me from any full exposition of our differences have also long since ceased to apply. Nevertheless, I still believe to this day that Lukács and I are objectively on the same side in our critical attitude towards the old Social Democratic Marxist orthodoxy and the new Communist orthodoxy. This is, after all, the central issue.

II

Marxism and Philosophy advanced a conception of Marxism that was quite *undogmatic and anti-dogmatic, historical and critical, and which was therefore materialist in the strictest sense of the word.* This conception involved *the application of the materialist conception of history to the materialist conception of history itself.* The orthodox critics of both old and new schools opposed this. Yet their first dogmatic counter-attack came in the guise of an extremely 'historical' and apparently quite 'undogmatic' accusation. They charged that my work showed a quite unjustified preference for the 'primitive' form in which Marx and Engels had originally founded their new dialectical materialist method, as a revolutionary theory that was directly related to revolutionary practice. I was alleged to have ignored the positive development of their theory by the Marxists of the Second International; and to have also completely overlooked the fact that Marx and Engels themselves had modified their original theory in important ways, so that it was only in a later form that it achieved its full historical elaboration.

It is clear that this raises an issue of really major importance for the historical materialist view of Marxist theory. It concerns the successive *phases of development* through which Marxism has passed from its original conception up to the situation today, where it is split into different historical versions. It also involves the *relationship* of these different phases to each other and their significance for the general historical development of theory in the modern working-class movement.

It is perfectly obvious that these different historical phases are bound to be evaluated in quite different ways by each of the dogmatic 'Marxist' tendencies which compete with each other in the socialist movement of today and which, even on the theoretical level, clash with greatest bitterness The collapse of the First International in the 1870s prefigured the collapse of the pre-1914 version of the Second International on the outbreak of the World War, in that both produced not one but several different tendencies, all of them invoking Marx and fighting each other for the 'genuine ring' – the right to claim the succession of true 'Marxism'. It is best simply to cut through the Gordian knot of these dogmatic disputes and place oneself on the terrain of a dialectical analysis. This can be expressed symbolically by saying that the real ring has been lost. In other words, *dogmatic* calculations of how far the different versions of Marxist theory correspond to some abstract canon of 'pure and unfalsified' theory should be abandoned. All these earlier and later Marxist ideologies must on the contrary be seen in a *historical, materialist and dialectical perspective* as products of a historical evolution. The way one defines the different phases of this evolution, and their relations to each other, will depend on the angle from which one starts such an analysis. In my work, there is a discussion of *the connection between Marxism and philosophy*, and for this purpose I have distinguished *three major periods of development* through which Marxism has passed *since* its birth and in each of which its relation to philosophy has changed in a specific way.[4] This particular approach is valid only for the history of *Marxism and Philosophy*. This is particularly true for the second period I distinguished, which is too undifferentiated for other purposes. I dated this second period from the battle of June 1848 and the subsequent years of the 1850s, which saw an unprecedented new upswing in capitalism and the crushing of all the proletarian organizations and dreams that had arisen in the previous epoch. In my schema, this period lasted up to about the turn of the century.

4. Kautsky (op. cit., p. 312) thinks that the 'primitive Marxism' that I and all other Communist theoreticians supposedly alone acknowledge consists of the theory found 'in the early works that Marx and Engels wrote before they were thirty'. Bammel, however, who follows Kautsky quite blindly in all other respects (op. cit., pp. 13ff.) irrelevantly applies his own erudition (ibid., p. 14) to attack me for ignorance because I 'began Marx's intellectual biography with the 1843 *Critique of Hegel's Philosophy of Right*'. It is enough to point out to both of them that I emphasized that Marxist theory had gone through these periods *after* its original emergence and that I considered the ideological expression of the *first* of these to be not the 'early works' but the works written after the *Critique of Hegel's Philosophy of Right*.

It would be quite possible to argue that this was too abstract a way of analysing the ties between Marxism and philosophy. For it involved treating an extremely long period as a single unity, and ignoring historical changes within it that were of great importance for the whole history of the workers' movement. Yet it is undoubtedly true that in the whole of the second half of the nineteenth century there was no such decisive change in the relationship between Marxism and philosophy as that which occurred at the mid-century. For it was then that philosophy expired, affecting the whole of the German bourgeoisie, and in a different way the proletariat as well. However, a full history of the relationship between Marxist theory and philosophy after 1850 would naturally have to make certain other major distinctions in this period, if it were not to be content with tracing only the very general outlines of the process. In this respect my work did leave open a great number of questions. Yet as far as I know they have not been broached by anyone else. For example, in a famous passage at the end of his work *Ludwig Feuerbach and the End of Classical German Philosophy*, Friedrich Engels refers in 1888 to the German workers' movement as the '*heir of classical German philosophy*'. This might have been taken as more than just the first sign of the approaching third phase, when Marxism and philosophy began to interact positively once again. For Engels himself refers in his introduction to 'a kind of rebirth of classical German philosophy abroad, in England and Scandinavia, and even in Germany itself' – although this at first only involved the revisionist Kantian Marxists who were applying the bourgeois slogan 'Back to Kant' to Marxist theory. I described the dialectical materialist, critical revolutionary theory of Marx and Engels in the 1840s as an '*anti-philosophy*' which yet in itself remained philosophical. It would be necessary to make a retrospective analysis of the four decades from 1850 to 1890 to show how this 'anti-philosophy' later developed in two separate directions. On the one hand, socialist 'science' became 'positive' and gradually turned away from philosophy altogether. On the other hand, a philosophical development occurred, apparently in conflict with the former but in fact complementary to it. This is first to be found in the late 1850s, in the writings of Marx and Engels themselves, and then later in those of their best disciples – Labriola in Italy and Plekhanov in Russia. Its theoretical character may be defined as a kind of return to Hegel's *philosophy* and not just a return to the essentially critical and revolutionary 'anti-philosophy' of the Left Hegelians in the *Sturm und Drang* period of the 1840s.[5]

This philosophical tendency of the later theory of Marx and Engels is not just to be found in the altered attitude to philosophy in Engels's *Feuerbach*. It also had definite implications for the further development of Marxist *economics*: clear signs of this are already present in Marx's 1859 *Critique of Political Economy* and in *Capital*. It had even more evident consequences for Engels's special topic of *the natural sciences*: they may be seen in his *Dialectics of Nature* and *Anti-Dühring*. Given all this, one can only regard the 'German workers' movement' as the 'heir of classical German philosophy' in so far as it 'absorbed' Marxist theory as a whole, including its philosophical aspects, with the birth of the Second International.

But these are not the issues raised by those who have criticized the three periods I outlined in the history of Marxism.

5. On this 'second' return to Hegel by Marx and Engels after the end of the 1850s, see some interesting points in Ryazanov, *Marx-Engels Archiv*, II, pp. 122ff. Labriola and Plekhanov developed this Hegelian philosophical trend, which is to be found in every line of their writings. It also persisted in Plekhanov's philosophical pupil, Lenin, in a specific form which will be discussed later.

They have not tried to show that this periodization was useless even for the specific purposes of my investigation. They prefer to accuse me of tending to present the whole history of Marxism after 1850 in a negative light, as a single, linear and univocal process of *decay suffered by the original revolutionary theory* of Marx and Engels – not only in the domain of the relation of Marxism to philosophy, but in every domain.[6] They love to attack this position, though I have never adopted it. They compete with each other in pointing out the absurdity of a view they themselves have invented and attributed to me; that Marx and Engels were responsible for the degeneration of their own theory. They never tire of proving the undoubtedly positive nature of the process that led from the original revolutionary Communism of the *Manifesto* to the 'Marxism of the First International' and then to the Marxism of *Capital* and the later writings of Marx and Engels. Having first argued that the later Marx and Engels made a significant contribution to the development of Marxist theory, which no one denies, they end by slipping into a claim that the 'Marxists of the Second International' made a 'positive' contribution to it too. This is where it becomes obvious that there was a *dogmatic preconception* behind these attacks from

6. To prove this accusation, Kautsky quotes two phrases he has taken out of their context, in footnotes 30 and 68; and he omits the sentence in which I made my position on this issue unambiguously clear and where it is placed in the general context of my argument (p. 30ff.). I explicitly characterized the later 'scientific socialism of the *Capital* of 1867–94 and of other later works by Marx and Engels' as a '*more developed manifestations of Marx's general theory*' compared to the 'immediately revolutionary communism' of the previous historical epoch. Further instances of my extremely positive attitude to the later and more developed form of their theory can be found in, for example, my introduction to Marx's 1875 *Critique of the Gotha Programme* and my article on 'The Marxism of the First International' in *Die Internationale*, 1924, pp. 573f.

the outset, though they all pretend to be concerned with the historical accuracy of my account of the development of Marxism after 1850. What this really involves is a straightforward dogmatic *defence of the traditional and orthodox thesis that the theory of the Second International was basically Marxist all along* (*according to Kautsky*) *or at any rate until the 'original sin' of* 4 *August* 1914 (*according to the Communists*).

Kautsky is the clearest example of orthodox Marxist prejudices about the real historical development of Marxism. For him, it is not only the theoretical metamorphoses of the different Marxist tendencies of the Second International, but the 'extension of Marxism undertaken by Marx and Engels with the *Inaugural Address* of 1864 and concluded with Engels's introduction to the new edition of Marx's *Class Struggles in France* in 1895' which 'broadened' Marxism from a theory of proletarian revolution into a 'theory valid not only for revolutionary phases but also for non-revolutionary periods'. At this stage, Kautsky had only robbed Marxist theory of its essentially revolutionary character: he still, however, professed to regard it as a 'theory of class struggle'. Later he went much further. His most recent major work, *The Materialist Conception of History*, eliminates any essential connection between Marxist theory and proletarian struggle whatever. His whole protest against my alleged 'charge' that Marx and Engels impoverished and banalized Marxism is merely a cover for a scholastic and dogmatic attempt to base his own betrayal of Marxism on the 'authority' of Marx and Engels. He and others once made a pretence of accepting Marxist theory, but have long since denatured it out of recognition, and have now abandoned the last remnants of it.

Yet it is exactly here that the theoretical solidarity of the new Communists with the old Marxist orthodoxy of Social Democracy emerges. Communist critics like Bammel argue that in my work 'concepts like "the Marxism of the Second International" are obscured by an excessively abstract and schematized problematic'. This accusation conceals a dogmatic attempt to defend the 'Marxism of the Second International' whose spiritual legacy Lenin and his companions never abandoned, in spite of some things they said in the heat of battle. As Communist 'theoreticians' tend to do in such cases, Bammel avoids taking any responsibility himself for trying to rescue the honour of Second International Marxism. Instead he hides in Lenin's ample shadow. He tries to explain to the reader what he means by attacking the allegedly 'abstract and schematic' way in which *Marxism and Philosophy* obscures the 'Marxism of the Second International', and he does this in standard scholastic fashion by quoting a sentence of Lenin in which he once acknowledged the 'historical contribution of the Second International' to advancing the modern workers' movement.[7] Lenin was a great tactician and

7. The phrase comes from a text Lenin wrote before the Lucerne Congress of the Berne International in July 1919 (*Collected Works*, vol. 29, pp. 494ff., 'The Tasks of the Third International'). It was a reply to an article written by the English Labour leader Ramsay MacDonald, at that time still considered to be a left socialist, about the 'Third International' – which had just then emerged before the eyes of the proletariat with its founding manifesto. MacDonald's article was published in German in the magazine *Die Kommunistische Internationale* (No. 4 and 5, pp. 52ff.), which at that time was issued by the West European secretariat of the Communist International. Bammel quotes this 'passage' to justify a completely different proposition, because in the specific context where it occurs in Lenin it does not refer at all to the Marxist theory of the Second International. All that Lenin cites as the 'historical service' and 'lasting achievement' of the Second International which 'no class conscious worker can deny' are such completely practical things as 'the organization of the working masses' the creation of co-operative trade union and political mass organizations, the use of bourgeois parliamentarianism as of all the institutions of bourgeois democracy and a lot more' (ibid., p. 504).

he made this remark in a highly complex tactical situation, when he was referring to the International's practical contribution and not to its theoretical one. But Bammel stops short of his intention of extending Lenin's praise of the good aspects of Social Democratic practice to Social Democratic theory. Instead of drawing this clear conclusion, he mumbles in 'an excessively abstract and obscure way' something to the effect that 'it would not be difficult to show that it would be quite possible to say somewhat the same thing about the theoretical foundation of Marxism'.

Since *Marxism and Philosophy* I have written a study elsewhere of the real historical nature of the 'Marxism of the Second International'. What happened was that the socialist movement reawoke and grew stronger as historical conditions changed over the last third of the nineteenth century; yet contrary to what is supposed, it never *adopted Marxism as a total system.*[8] According to the ideology of the orthodox Marxists and of their opponents, who share much the same dogmatic ground, it is to be believed that the *whole of Marxism* was adopted in both theory and practice. In fact all that was even theoretically adopted were some isolated economic, political and social 'theories', extracted from the general context of revolutionary Marxism. Their general meaning had thereby been altered; and their specific content usually truncated and falsified. The endless asseverations of *the rigorously*

8. See my book, issued by the publishers of this text, *Die materialistische Geschichtsauffassung. Eine Auseinandersetzung mit Karl Kautsky* ('The Materialist Conception of History. A Dispute with Karl Kautsky', hereafter referred to as *Auseinandersetzung mit Kautsky*) and especially the last section on 'The Historical Significance of Kautskyism' (which was *not* included in the shortened version printed in Grünberg's *Archiv für die Geschichte des Sozialismus und der Arbeiterbewegung*, XIV, pp. 197ff.).

'Marxist' character of the programme and theory of the movement do not date from the period in which the practice of the new Social Democratic workers' movement approximated most to the revolutionary and class-combative character of Marxist theory. In this early period the 'two old men in London', and after Marx's death in 1883, Friedrich Engels alone, were directly involved in the movement. Paradoxically, these asseverations date from a *later* period when certain other tendencies were gaining ground in both trade union and political practice, which were ultimately to find their ideological expression in 'revisionism'. In fact, at the time when the practice of the movement was most revolutionary, its theory was essentially 'populist' and democratic (under the influence of Lassalle and Dühring) and only sporadically 'Marxist'.[9] This was the result of the impact of the periods of economic crisis and depression in the 1870s the political and social reaction following the defeat of the Paris Commune in 1871, the Anti-socialist laws in Germany, the defeat of the growing socialist movement in Austria in 1884 and the violent suppression of the movement for an eight-hour day in America in 1886. However, the 1890s saw a new industrial boom in Europe, especially in Germany, and therewith the first signs appeared of a 'more democratic' use of state power on the continent of Europe. This process included the French amnesty for the Communards in 1880, and the lapsing of the anti-socialist laws in Germany in 1890. In this new practical context, *formal avowals of the Marxist system as a whole*

9. Cf. the correspondence of Marx and Engels from that period, printed in my edition of Marx's *Critique of the Gotha Programme* (and in Marx and Engels, *Selected Works*, vol. II, pp. 13ff.), and the relevant remarks in my introduction, pp. 6ff. Further important materials for clarifying this relationship are contained in Friedrich Engels's *Letters to Bernstein*, 1881–1895, which have subsequently appeared (Berlin, 1925).

emerged as a kind of theoretical defence and metaphysical consolation. In this sense, one can actually invert the generally accepted relationship between Kautskyian 'Marxism' and Bernsteinian 'revisionism', and define Kautsky's *orthodox Marxism* as the theoretical obverse and symmetrical complement of *Bernstein's revisionism.*[10]

In the light of this real historical situation, the complaints of orthodox Marxist critics against my work are not only unjustified but null and void. I am alleged to have a predilection for the 'primitive' form of the first historical version of the theory of Marx and Engels, and to have disregarded its positive development by Marx and Engels themselves, and by other Marxists in the second half of the nineteenth century. It is claimed that the 'Marxism of the Second International' represents an advance on original Marxist theory. Yet in fact it was *a new historical form of proletarian class theory*, which emerged from the altered practical context of the class struggle in a new historical epoch. Its relationship to the earlier or later versions of the theory of Marx and Engels is very different from, and essentially more complex than, the way it is presented by those who talk of a *positive development*, or conversely of a *formal stagnation* or *regression and decay* of Marx's theory in the 'Marxism of the Second International'. Marxism is therefore in no way a socialist theory that has been 'superseded' by the present outlook of the workers' movement, as Kautsky maintains (formally he refers only to its

10. Cf. the matching accounts now given by Bernstein and Kautsky of the changes that took place at this time, both in their individual relationships to Marxist theory, and in their theoretical relationship to each other. This completely corrects the legend that Social Democratic theory had an explicitly and emphatically 'Marxist' character before Bernstein 'revised it'; in Meiner's *Volkswirtschaftslehre in Selbstdarstellungen*, Leipzig, 1924, pp. 12ff. (Bernstein) and pp. 134ff. (Kautsky).

earlier version, the 'primitive Marxism of the Communist Manifesto', but actually he includes all the later components of Marx and Engels's theory as well). Nor is Marxism what it was claimed to be by the representatives of the revolutionary tendency within orthodox Social Democratic Marxism at the start of the third period towards 1900, or what some Marxists still consider it to be. It is not a theory that has miraculously anticipated the future development of the workers' movement for a long time to come. Consequently it cannot be said that the subsequent practical progress of the proletariat has, as it were, lagged behind its own theory or that it will only gradually come to occupy the framework allotted to it by this theory.[11] When the SPD became a 'Marxist' party (a

11. In spite of his famous statement that he was 'not a Marxist', Marx himself was not entirely free from this somewhat dogmatic and idealist conception of the relationship of his Marxist theory to later manifestations of the working-class movement. See for example his repeated complaints in the 1875 *Critique of the Gotha Programme* about the scandalous theoretical regressions of the draft programme in comparison to the superior understanding that had previously been attained and about the way the authors of the programme had 'monstrously violated the views held by the Party masses'. Later radical-left opponents of revisionism and of centrist Orthodox Marxism formally converted this attitude in to a system. They then claimed Marxism had 'stagnated' and used this system to explain why. For example, Rosa Luxemburg in an article in *Vorwärts*, 14 March 1903, states in all seriousness that the 'theoretical stagnation' which can now be detected in the movement has not occurred 'because our practical struggles have surpassed Marxism but on the contrary because Marx's theoretical achievement is in advance of *us* as a practical militant party. It is not because Marx is no longer adequate for our needs. but because our needs are not yet adequate to profit from Marx's thought'. The learned Marxist Ryazanov reprinted this article of Rosa Luxemburg's in a collection that was published in German in 1928 (English edition, *Karl Marx – Man, Thinker, and Revolutionist*, London, 1927, pp. 105ff.). Although Rosa Luxemburg's piece was written almost thirty years ago, he has only the following to add to it from the vantage-point of today: 'The practical experience of the Russian Revolution has shown that every new stage in the develop-

process completed with the Erfurt Programme written by Kautsky and Bernstein in 1891) a gap developed between its highly articulated revolutionary 'Marxist' theory and a practice that was far behind this revolutionary theory; in some respects it directly contradicted it. This gap was in fact obvious, and it later came to be felt more and more acutely by all the vital forces in the Party (whether on the Left or Right) and its existence was denied only by the orthodox Marxists of the Centre. This gap can easily be explained by the fact that in this historical phase 'Marxism', while formally accepted by the workers' movement, was from the start not a true *theory*, in the sense of being 'nothing other than a general expression of the real historical movement' (Marx). On the contrary it was always an *ideology* that had been adopted 'from outside' in a pre-established form.

In this situation such 'orthodox Marxists' as Kautsky and Lenin made a permanent virtue out of a temporary necessity. They energetically defended the idea that socialism can only be brought to the workers 'from outside', by bourgeois intellectuals who are allied to the workers' movement.[12] This

---

ment of the class struggle of the proletariat discloses in the inexhaustible arsenal of Marxist theory the new weapons that are needed for the new phase of the struggle' (ibid., pp. 11–12). Rosa Luxemburg turned the relation of theory to practice on its head; this dictum has certainly not put it back on its feet again.

12. Cf. Kautsky's polemic in *Neue Zeit*, XX, I, pp. 68ff. against the draft for a new version of the Hainfeld Programme, submitted to the Vienna Party Congress of 1901. In one passage this draft stated that the prolatariat comes to *consciousness* of the possibility and necessity of socialism through the struggles that are forced on it by capitalist development. Kautsky summed up the meaning of this very well: it meant that 'socialist consciousness appears as the necessary and direct result of the proletariat struggle'. He goes on to say: 'But this is not true. Socialism as a theory is of course as rooted in modern economic conditions as is the struggle of the proletariat, and both arise equally

was also true of Left radicals like Rosa Luxemburg who talked of the 'stagnation of Marxism' and explained it by contrasting Marx to the proletariat: the one had creative power because he was armed with all the resources of a bourgeois education, while the other remains tied to 'the social conditions of existence in our society', which will continue un-

---

from the struggle against the mass poverty and mass misery which capitalism produces. But they arise parallel to one another and not out of each other, and they do so under different conditions. Modern socialist consciousness can only arise on the basis of profound scientific understanding, and modern economic knowledge is in fact as much a precondition for socialist production as is modern technology. But with the best will in the world the proletariat can create neither one nor the other; both arise out of the contemporary social process. However the bearer of science is not the proletariat but the *bourgeois intelligentsia*. Modern socialism first emerged among certain members of this group and through them was first conveyed to the intellectually advanced proletarians. They then introduced it into class struggle, where conditions permitted. Socialist consciousness is therefore something that is brought into proletarian struggle from the outside and not something that grew naturally from within it. The old Hainfeld Programme was therefore quite right to say that it was the task of Social Democracy to introduce the proletariat to the *consciousness* of their condition and of their tasks. That would not be necessary if this consciousness could emerge spontaneously from class struggle' (ibid., pp. 79ff.). A year later, in 1902, Lenin in his famous programme *What is to be Done?* developed the key points in Kautsky's arguments. He reprints the whole of what he considers to be these '*extremely striking and important words of Kautsky's*' and draws the explicit conclusion that 'one cannot talk of an autonomous ideology formulated by the working masses themselves in the course of their movement' (*Collected Works*, vol. 5, pp. 383–4). The same thesis is found in many other parts of the book, e.g. p. 375, in the following quite unambiguous phrases: 'The history of all countries shows that the working class, exclusively by its own effort, is able to develop only trade-union consciousness, i.e. the conviction that it is necessary to combine in unions, fight the employers, and strive to compel the government to pass necessary labour legislation, etc. The theory of socialism, however, grew out of the philosophical, historical and economic theories elaborated by the educated representatives of the propertied classes, by intellectuals.'

altered throughout the capitalist epoch.[13] The truth is that a *historical fact* provides a materialist explanation of this apparent contradiction between theory and practice in the 'Marxist' Second International, and a rational solution for all the mysteries which the orthodox Marxists of that time devised to explain it. The fact is this. The workers' movement at that time formally adopted 'Marxism' as its ideology; yet although its effective practice was now on a *broader basis* than before, it had in no way reached the *heights* of general and theoretical achievement earlier attained by the revolutionary movement and proletarian class struggle on a *narrower basis.* This height was attained during the final phase of the firs major capitalist cycle that came to an end towards 1850. At that time, the workers' movement had achieved a peak of development. But it then came to a temporary yet complete halt, and only revived slowly, as conditions changed. Marx and Engels had initially conceived their revolutionary theory in direct relation to the practical revolutionary movement, but when this died down they could only continue their work as theory. It is true that this later development of Marxist theory was never just the production of 'purely theoretical' study; it was always a theoretical reflection of the latest practical experiences of the class struggle which was reawakening in

13. Ryazanov, op. cit., p. 113. Leon Trotsky's *Literature and Revolution*, which appeared in Russian at the end of 1923 and in German a year later (published by Verlag für Literatur und Politik, Vienna, 1924), contains a curious repetition and development of this Luxemburgist thesis that the working class 'will be in a position to create their own science and art only after being completely liberated from their present class situation', and that it is only in socialist society that the Marxist method of analysis, in particular, will become the full property of the proletariat – which in any case will cease to exist as such (*Literature and Revolution*, Ann Arbor, 1960, pp. 146–7 and pp. 184ff. and especially pp. 196 ff.).

various ways. Nevertheless it is clear that the *theory* of Marx and Engels was progressing towards an ever higher level of theoretical perfection although it was no longer directly related to the *practice* of the worker's movement. Thus two processes unfolded side by side in relative independence of each other. One was the *development under novel conditions of the old theory which had arisen in a previous historical epoch.* The other was the *new practice of the workers' movement.* It is this which explains the literally 'anachronistic' height which Marxist theory reached and surpassed in this period, generally and philosophically, in the work of Marx, Engels and some of their disciples. This is also why it was wholly impossible for this highly elaborate Marxist theory to be effectively and not just formally assimilated by the proletarian movement, whose practice reawakened during the last third of the nineteenth century.[14]

III

Orthodox Marxists, whether Social Democrats or Communists, have a second major criticism. This concerns my thesis in *Marxism and Philosophy* that there needs to be a new appraisal of the relation between philosophy and Marxism in the *third phase of the development of Marxism* which began at the turn of the century. In the period before this, various trends within Marxism had neglected and minimized the revolutionary philosophical content of the teaching of Marx and Engels – a neglect which took various forms but had a common outcome. By contrast, *Marxism and Philosophy* aimed

14. This is discussed in more detail in my *Auseinandersetzung mit Kautsky*, pp. 119ff.

to re-emphasize this *philosophical side of Marxism.* In doing so it stood opposed to all those groups within German and international Marxism which had earlier appeared as consciously Kantian, Machian or other philosophical 'revisions' of Marxism. The most prominent of these trends, which developed among the dominant centrist group within Orthodox Marxist Social Democracy, came more and more to adopt an *anti-philosophical, scientifico-positivist conception of Marxism.* Even such orthodox revolutionaries as Franz Mehring paid tribute to this view by endorsing its disdain for all philosophical 'fantasies'. Nevertheless, it soon became clear that my conception of the revolutionary tasks of philosophy today was if possible even more antagonistic to a *third trend.* This was a tendency which had mainly emerged from the two factions of Russian Marxism and was now chiefly represented by the theoreticians of the new Bolshevik 'Marxism-Leninism'.

Both Georg Lukács's studies on dialectical materialism and the first edition of my own work appeared in 1923. As soon as they became known, they were attacked with extraordinary hostility by the Party press in Russia and everywhere else. This was mainly due to the fact that the leadership of the Russian Party, under the slogan of 'propagating Leninism', had by then begun their campaign to 'Bolshevize' the ideology of all the non-Russian Parties that belonged to the Communist International.[15] This coincided with a sharpening of the struggle among Lenin's successors for the legacy of Leninism (which had begun during his lifetime), and with the events of October and November 1923 in Germany which constituted a major defeat for the political practice of international

15. Cf. my programmatic article 'Lenin and the Comintern', published in the theoretical journal of the German Communist Party, *Die Internationale* (1924, pp. 320ff.) on the coming Fifth World Congress of the Communist International.

Communism in the West. The central element of this 'Bolshevized' ideology was a strictly *philosophical* ideology that claimed to restore the true unfalsified philosophy of Marx. On this basis, it aimed to combat all other philosophical tendencies within the workers' movement.

As it moved westwards, this Marxist-Leninist philosophy encountered the works of Lukács, myself and other 'Western' Communists which formed *an antagonistic philosophical tendency within the Communist International itself.* This then led to the first real and direct philosophical discussion between the two revolutionary trends that had developed within the pre-war Social Democratic International. These were united only superficially in the Communist International, although their disagreements had hitherto been confined to political and tactical questions.[16] For certain historical reasons to be mentioned below, this philosophical discussion was only a weak echo of the political and tactical disputes that the two sides had conducted so fiercely some years before. It was soon obscured by the factional disputes that from 1925 onwards emerged in the Russian Party and which were then fought out more and more fiercely in all the other Communist Parties. In spite of this, the discussion did have a certain importance for a time within the overall development. For it was a first attempt to break through what a Russian critic, who was extremely well informed on the theoretical situation on both sides, called the 'mutual impenetrability' that had hitherto prevailed between

16. Here one might recall the strong criticism by Rosa Luxemburg and Karl Liebknecht of Bolshevik politics and tactics, dating from the very first period after the Russian Revolution and before the formal establishment of the Communist International; also the disagreement that culminated in the years 1920–1 between the radical left tendency led by the Dutch Communists Pannekoek and Gorter and the Russian Bolshevik faction led by Lenin.

the ideological positions of Russian and of Western Communism.[17]

Let us sum up this *philosophical dispute of* 1924 in the *ideological form* that it took in the minds of those who participated in it. It was a dispute between, on the one hand, the Leninist interpretation of Marx and Engels's materialism[18] which had

17. Cf. the analysis of 'Soviet Marxism' by Max Werner (A. Schifrin) in *Die Gesellschaft*, IV, 7, pp. 42ff. and especially pp. 60ff. This is a comprehensive study, which is especially informative for non-Russian readers as it makes use of documents that are available only in Russian. While it must be borne in mind that this critical comparison of Russian and Western Marxism comes from a *political opponent* of the party in power in Russia today, its author is nevertheless an orthodox Plekhanovite and is philosophically on the side of Russian Marxism. Consequently his criticism is not at all aimed against the general historical structure of 'Soviet Marxism', but only against its latest caricatured forms which make it appear to be not a 'development and continuation', but a 'corruption and distortion' of the theoretical traditions of Russian Marxism. ('It is self-evident that Plekhanov bears no responsibility for Soviet Marxism'.) Schifrin has only a very superficial and ideological understanding of why 'it is so difficult, if not impossible for West European Communists and – more generally – for all European Left Marxists, for all those who have been reared in (for example) the theoretical traditions of Rosa Luxemburg and Franz Mehring, to enter into the spirit of Russian Marxism'. On the one hand he ascribes this in a purely ideological way to the fact that radical Left Marxism in the West 'did not have the enlightenment traditions of Russian Marxism behind it'. On the other hand he locates its origin superficially in the 'fact that Soviet Marxism has been very specifically formed as a state ideology' and 'tailored to the very specific tasks of the Soviet state'. On pp. 63ff. he invokes certain historical and class factors to explain the conflicts between the *political theory* of West European Marxism and of the left radicalism that preceded it on the one hand, and that of Russian Bolshevism on the other. But he fails to grasp that these are also the real and more profound causes of the *theoretical* and *ideological* disagreements between Russian and West European Marxism.

18. Cf. two little works by A. Deborin which appeared as early as 1924: *Lenin the Fighting Materialist* and *Lenin's Letters to Maxim Gorki*, as well as the German translation of Lenin's programmatic text

already been formally canonized in Russia and, on the other hand, what were alleged to be views that 'deviated' from this canon in the direction of idealism, of Kant's critical epistemology and of Hegel's idealist dialectic. These were the views of George Lukács and a number of other theoreticians in the German and Hungarian Communist Parties who were regarded with varying degrees of justice as his supporters.[19]

In the case of *Marxism and Philosophy*, this accusation of an 'idealist deviation' was partially based on attributions to the author of views which he had never expressed in his work: in

---

Materialism and Empirio-Criticism: Critical Comments on a Reactionary Philosophy which appeared *post festum* with a delay of three years, in 1927 (*Collected Works*, vol. 14, pp. 17ff.). J. Luppol's *Lenin and Philosophy: On the Question of the Relationship of Philosophy to Revolution* (in Russian) is a belated contribution to this literature – a wretched little pamphlet.

19. See for example Deborin's philosophical anti-critique of the views expressed by Lukács in *History and Class Consciousness* which appeared at that time ('Lukács and his Critique of Marxism' in the periodical *Arbeiterliteratur*, No. 10, pp. 615ff., published by Verlag für Literatur und Politik, Vienna, 1924), and the presentation there (p. 618) of the way in which the leading representatives of philosophical 'Leninism' saw things at that time: 'Lukács already has his disciples and is in a certain sense the leading figure of a whole movement to which belong, among others: comrades Korsch (see his book *Marxism and Philosophy*), Fogarasi, Révai and others. Given the way things are, one cannot ignore them. At the very least we must submit the basic principles of this "new trend" in Marxism to criticism.' See also similar statements in *Pravda*, 25 July 1924: 'Lukács's book must attract the attention of Marxist critics because behind Lukács there is a whole group of Communists: K. Korsch, Révai, Fogarasi and others' – and further: 'K. Korsch belongs to the group of German Communist comrades whom comrade Zinoviev at the Fifth World Congress mentioned in passing as theoreticians who deviate from the orthodox Marxist line in philosophy.' Much the same is found in most other theoreticians who took part in the campaign that was launched at that time in all Communist journals and papers against this new 'deviation'.

some cases he had explicitly rejected them, as in the case of his alleged denial of the 'dialectics of nature'.[20] However, attacks were also directed at views that really did occur in *Marxism and Philosophy*, and especially against its repeated dialectical rejection of 'naïve realism'. The latter included both 'so-called sound common sense, the worst metaphysician', and the normal 'positivist science' of bourgeois society; it also included the sad heir of positivism today, namely, a vulgar-marxism that is devoid of any philosophical perspective. For all these 'draw a sharp line of division between consciousness and its object' and 'treat consciousness as something given, something fundamentally contrasted to Being and Nature' (as Engels pointed out against Dühring as early as 1878).

Because I then believed that this view was *self-evident* to any materialist dialectician or revolutionary Marxist, I assumed rather than spelt out this critique of a *primitive, pre-dialectical and even pre-transcendental conception of the relation between consciousness and being*. But without realizing it I had hit on the very key to the 'philosophical' outlook which was then due to be dispensed from Moscow to the whole of the West-

20. This is actually stated in the *Pravda* article of 25 July 1924, already mentioned, and by most other Communist Party critics. Cf. the contrary position expounded in *Marxism and Philosophy* (pp. 30ff. above), which states the opposite of what I am alleged to hold. The same is true of the stereotyped and recurrent accusation made by Communist Party critics in this connection that I have made an *essential distinction between the views of Engels and those of Marx on this point*. In fact *Marxism and Philosophy* refrained in general and also with respect to this particular question (see note 75) from the one-sided fashion in which Lukács and Révai treated the views of Marx and Engels, as if they were completely at variance. It equally refrains from the fundamentally dogmatic and therefore unscientific procedure of the 'orthodox', who make it a completely self-evident and unshakeable article of faith that the 'doctrine' produced by the two Church Fathers was absolutely consistent.

ern Communist world. Indeed it formed the basis of the new orthodox theory, so-called 'Marxism-Leninism'. The professional exponents of the new Russian 'Marxism-Leninism' then replied to this supposedly 'idealist' attack by repeating the ABC of the 'materialist' alphabet they had learnt by heart.[21] This they did with a naïveté that can only appear as a 'state of philosophical innocence' to corrupt 'Westerners'.

I think that the specifically *theoretical debate* with Lenin's materialist philosophy, which Lenin's epigones have followed to the letter despite grotesque inconsistencies and crying contradictions in it, is itself of secondary importance. This is

21. 'The ABC of Marxist philosophy is that truth is defined as the agreement of a representation with the objects that are external to it. Korsch calls this "the naïve metaphysical standpoint of sound bourgeois common-sense". He does not understand, or want to understand, that it is precisely his (Korsch's) standpoint on this issue that is bourgeois – an idealist mixture of the philosophy of identity and of Machism' (*Pravda*, 25 July 1924). The same argument is expressed by the editor and critical commentator of the Russian translation of *Marxism and Philosophy*, Bammel. In his introduction (p. 19) he quotes verbatim my statements on the consequences of this 'naïve metaphysical standpoint of sound bourgeois common sense' for a theoretical and practical position on so-called 'more elevated ideologies' (p. 69 above). He then describes this whole passage and the reflections that follow it as 'totally incomprehensible' and poses the following accusatory question: 'Can Comrade Korsch be counted as a Marxist materialist if he regards as a "naïve metaphysical standpoint of bourgeois common sense" that view which defines truth as the agreement of a representation with an object that exists outside it and is "reflected" by it? Is it necessary to point out that his position on this question is a capitulation to the idealist theory of perception?' However, it is easy to reply to this crushing question by asking a contrary one: 'If that is so, why was such a terrible idealist book published in the first place?' Thus the penetrating critic suddenly remembers his responsibility as an editor and pleads extenuating circumstances: 'The nub of the problem is that Comrade Korsch is ignorant of the questions of gnoseology that affect the problem in which he is interested.'

because when he was alive Lenin himself did not base this philosophy on any essentially theoretical formulation. Instead, he defended it on practical and political grounds as the only philosophy that was 'beneficial' to the revolutionary proletariat. He contrasted it with 'harmful' systems derived from Kantian, Machian and other idealist philosophies. This attitude is clearly expressed in his intimate correspondence on 'philosophical' questions with Maxim Gorki in the years following the first Russian Revolution of 1905. Though they were personal friends, they disagreed philosophically and Lenin tried again and again to persuade Gorky that 'a member of the party has the duty to oppose a particular theory if he is convinced that it is completely incorrect and harmful', and that the most important thing to do in the case of such an 'absolutely unavoidable struggle' is 'to ensure that the essential practical work of the party *is not impaired*'.[22] Similarly the

22. The sentences quoted in the text are taken from a letter of Lenin's dated 24 March 1908 and the words italicized here were underlined by him. One can clearly see from this letter and from his later correspondence how Lenin as a 'party man' unreservedly subordinates all theoretical issues to party interest (*Collected Works*, vol. 34, pp. 388). However the Russian editor of the German translation of Lenin's *Materialism and Empirio-Criticism*, A. Deborin, is rewriting history when he tries to show that at that time there was a 'fundamental difference' between the public *tactical position* taken up by Lenin on these philosophical issues and the position held by such orthodox Marxists and materialists as Karl Kautsky. Even Lenin's letter to Gorki which has just been quoted and on which Deborin (ibid., pp. xixff.) bases his supposition, does not conclude with an open declaration of war but with a diplomatic proposal for 'conditional neutrality'; it was to be 'conditional' because '*it is essential to divorce this whole issue from the inner party dispute*.'

Moreover in the first edition of *Marxism and Philosophy*, note 6, we already reproduced the peculiar counter-statement which the editors of the Russian *Proletary* (Lenin) published at this time in the magazine Kautsky edited, *Neue Zeit* [10 March 1908], XXVI, 1, p. 898. This

real importance of *Lenin's major philosophical work* does not lie in the philosophical arguments he uses to combat and 'refute' the various idealist tendencies in modern bourgeois philosophy; of these Kantianism had influenced the revisionist tendency within the socialist movement of the period, while Machian 'empirio-criticism' had influenced the centrist tendency. The real importance of Lenin's work rests in the extreme rigour with which he tried in practice to combat and destroy these contemporary philosophical trends. He regarded them as *ideologies that were incorrect from the standpoint of party work.*

---

concerned a critical observation that had been printed in the previous issue on the philosophical differences within the Russian Social Democratic Party. Lenin then made the following official statement in the name of Bolshevik Social Democracy (*Collected Works*, vol. 13, pp. 447): 'This philosophical dispute (i.e. as had already been stated: "the question of whether Marxist epistemology agrees with Spinoza and Holbach, or with Mach and Avenarius"!) is not in fact an issue of inner party dispute and, in the opinion of the editors, it should not become so. Any attempt to construe these differences of opinion as the distinctive marks of the factions within the party is basically misguided. Among both factional groups there are supporters as well as opponents of Mach and Avenarius.'

This statement formally concurs with the critical observation in *Neue Zeit*, 14 February 1908; it too had described this philosophical dispute as an unnecessary sharpening of the 'extremely serious tactical differences between Bolsheviks and Mensheviks'. A year later Kautsky in a letter to the Russian emigré Bendianitse, 26 March 1909, suggested that within the Party Machism be declared a matter of individual choice. Deborin attacks this proposal violently as an 'evident absurdity for any Marxist'. Any objective historian, however, must point out that Lenin, in the two statements of the previous year already mentioned, 'declared Machism to be a matter of individual choice' not only *within the Party* but even within each *faction*. Moreover, a year later, at the Paris Conference of the 'Enlarged Editorial Board of the *Proletary*' (i.e. what amounted to the party leadership at that time) a split occurred that was not totally unconnected with these philosophical issues. It was not between Bolsheviks and Mensheviks, but *within the Bolshevik faction*

One vital point must be made here.[23] The author of this supposed restoration of the true materialist philosophy of Marx was quite clear about the kind of theoretical work Marx and Engels had carried out after finishing once and for all with the idealism of Hegel and the Hegelians in the 1840s:[24] 'They *limited* themselves in the field of epistemology to correcting the mistakes of Feuerbach, to mocking at the banalities of Dühring, to criticizing the mistakes of Büchner, and to emphasizing dialectics – which is what these authors, who were very popular in working-class circles, lacked *most of all*.' 'Marx, Engels and Dietzgen did not bother about the basic truths of materialism. These were being hawked around the world by dozens of pedlars. They concentrated on preventing

---

itself. On this occasion Lenin made an official reply to Bogdanov's declaration of a split in which he said that Bogdanov had split from the Bolshevik *faction* but not from the *party*: 'the faction is not a party and the party can contain within itself a wide range of shades of opinion of which the most extreme may be absolutely contradictory' (contained in vol. II, p. 329, note 2, in the French edition of Lenin's selected works which have been edited with a meticulous commentary by P. Pascal: V. I. Lenin, *Pages Choisies*, vols. I and II, Paris, 1926 and 1927; *Collected Works*, vol. 15, p. 430. So in fact Lenin and Kautsky formally held the same position on this issue and it is only later that the violent differences in their general outlook developed and became clear.

23. Cf. the section devoted to this in *Materialism and Empirio-Criticism* (pp. 238ff.) entitled 'Two Kinds of Criticism of Dühring', from which all the quoted passages are taken; the italics are Lenin's.

24. At this point Lenin does not distinguish *different periods in the development of Marx and Engels* as his text proposes to do; he merely talks in general of the period when 'both Marx and Engels as well as J. Dietzgen entered the philosophical arena' (ibid., p. 242). It is obvious, though, that he is referring to their position after the end of the 1850s. More important than this *chronological* division for judging different statements by Marx and Engels is a division by whom they were addressed to. *Marxism and Philosophy* includes a concrete discussion of the latter division.

these basic truths from being vulgarized and simplified too far, from leading to intellectual stagnation ("materialism below, idealism above"), and on preventing the *valuable* fruit of the idealist system, Hegel's dialectic, from being forgotten. These were the gems which idiots like Büchner, Dühring and co. (as well as Leclair, Mach, Avenarius, etc.) were unable to extract from the dungheap of absolute idealism.' To put it briefly: a result of the way existing historical conditions affected the philosophical work of Marx and Engels was that 'they tended *rather to distance* themselves from vulgarizations of basic materialist truths than to *defend* these truths themselves'. Similarly, in their political work 'they tended more to distance themselves from vulgar versions of the basic demands of political democracy than actually to defend these basic demands'. Lenin, however, argues that *present historical conditions are, in this respect, completely different.* He and all other revolutionary Marxists and materialists must now make it a leading priority to defend, not basic democratic political demands, but the 'basic truths of philosophical materialism' against their modern opponents in the bourgeois camp and their agents in the proletarian camp itself. These truths must be deliberately linked to the revolutionary bourgeois materialism of the seventeenth and eighteenth centuries, and spread among the millions and millions of peasants and other backward masses throughout Russia, Asia and the whole world.[25]

25. On this positive aspect of Lenin's materialist propaganda, see in particular Lenin's March 1922 article in the third issue of the Russian magazine *Under the Banner of Marxism.* A German translation appeared in the magazine *Kommunistische Internationale*, no. 21, and it was later reprinted in vol. I, Year 1 of the German edition of *Under the Banner of Marxism* in March 1925. It is particularly informative for correctly assessing the real historical significance of Lenin's materialism (*Collected Works*, vol. 33, pp. 227–36, 'On the Significance of Militant Materialism').

It is clear that Lenin is not primarily concerned with the *theoretical problem* of whether the materialist philosophy he propounds is true or untrue. He is concerned with the *practical question* of its use for the revolutionary struggle of the proletariat, or – in countries where capitalism is not fully developed – of the proletariat and other oppressed classes. Lenin's 'philosophical' standpoint basically appears, therefore, to be a specific, if disguised version of the position which in a different form had already been discussed in the first edition of *Marxism and Philosophy*. This position was strongly criticized by Marx as a young man when he wrote of the 'practically-oriented political party which imagines that it can supersede philosophy (in practice) without realizing it (in theory)'. Lenin decides philosophical questions *only* on the basis of non-philosophical considerations and results. He does not judge them on the basis of their theoretical and philosophical content *as well*. In so doing he commits the same mistakes as according to Marx the 'practically-oriented political party in Germany' committed. The latter believed it was accomplishing its justified aim of the 'negation of all philosophy' (in Lenin, of all idealist philosophy) because 'it turns its back on philosophy, looks in the other direction and mutters irritable and banal remarks about it'.[26]

26. *Critique of Hegel's Philosophy of Right* (*On Religion*, p. 48). This is not the place to show at greater length how Lenin's arguments against idealist philosophy largely fall into this category of Marx's. We will just cite one argument to *illustrate* this. Lenin 'refutes' the transcendentalist philosophical theory of the relation of subject and object in experience, by invoking the former molten state of the earth when there could be no subjective 'representations' of it. Lenin brings out this rather extraordinary philosophical argument again and again in various forms in the section of his work specifically concerned with this issue (op. cit., pp. 75ff., 'Did Nature Exist Prior to Man?'). However, it is not only Lenin who uses it, but also his materialist and philosophical predeces-

Any discussion of Lenin's position on philosophy and ideology must pose one initial question on which a judgement of Lenin's specific 'materialist philosophy' has to depend. According to a principle established by Lenin himself, this question is a *historical* one. Lenin argued that there had been a change in the whole intellectual climate which made it necessary when dealing with dialectical materialism to stress *materialism* against certain fashionable tendencies in bourgeois philosophy, rather than to stress *dialectics* against the vulgar, pre-dialectical and in some cases explicitly undialectical and anti-dialectical materialism of bourgeois science. The question is whether there had been such a change. What I have written elsewhere shows that I do not think this is really the case. There are some superficial aspects of contemporary bourgeois philosophy and science which appear to contradict this, and there certainly are some trends which genuinely do so. Nevertheless the dominant *basic trend* in contemporary bourgeois philosophy, natural science and humanities is the same as it was sixty or seventy years ago. It is inspired not by an idealist outlook but by *a materialist outlook that is coloured by the natural sciences*.[27] Lenin's position, which disputes this, is

---

sor Plekhanov. Instead of invoking the 'molten earth', Plekhanov says that the modern 'secondary epoch' began with the 'subjective categories of the ichthyosaurus'. A one-sided reading of Engels's famous 'alizarin argument' against 'Kant's unintelligible things-in-themselves' in the second section of *Ludwig Feuerbach* would also include it in this category. Cf. Lenin, op. cit., pp. 82, 87, and the statements by Plekhanov and Engels quoted there by Lenin.

27. Cf. my more detailed exposition in *Auseinandersetzung mit Kautsky* (pp. 29ff.) and in Grünberg's *Archiv für die Geschichte des Sozialismus und der Arbeiterbewegung*, vol. XIV, pp. 205ff. One should add that when Lenin continually claims there has been a new shift of early bourgeois materialism into idealism and agnosticism, he invokes Engels's 1892 Introduction to the English translation of *Die Entwicklung des Sozialismus von der Utopie zur Wissenschaft*. However, this outstand-

in close ideological relation to his politico-economic theory of 'imperialism'. Both have their *material roots* in the specific economic and social situation of Russia and the specific practical and theoretical political tasks that seemed, and for a short period really were, necessary to accomplish the Russian Revolution. This means that the 'Leninist' theory is not theoretically capable of answering the *practical needs of the international class struggle in the present period.* Consequently, Lenin's materialist philosophy, which forms the ideological basis of this theory, cannot constitute the revolutionary proletarian philosophy that will answer the needs of today.

The *theoretical character* of Lenin's materialist philosophy also corresponds to this historical and practical situation. Like Plekhanov, his philosophical master, and L. Axelrod-Orthodox, the latter's other philosophical pupil, Lenin wanted very seriously to be a *Marxist* while remaining a *Hegelian.* He thereby flouted the dialectical materialist outlook that Marx and Engels founded at the start of their revolutionary development. This outlook was by its very nature unavoidably 'philosophical', but it pointed towards the complete supersession of philosophy; and it left one single revolutionary task in the philosophical field, which was to develop this outlook by taking it to a higher level of elaboration. Lenin regards the transition from Hegel's idealist dialectic to Marx and Engels's dialectical materialism as nothing more than an *exchange*: the

---

ing text (it was published in German in *Neue Zeit*, XI, 1, and has now been reprinted in the new edition of Engels's work on Ludwig Feuerbach, Berlin and Vienna, 1927) does not consider the new bourgeois idealism and agnosticism to be the major theoretical danger faced by the revolutionary workers' movement. Engels describes it quite bluntly as a 'miserable materialism' and with magisterial disdain he mocks at the hopes which the bourgeoisie attach to such ideological ramparts. (*Selected Works*, vol. II, pp. 93ff.).

idealist outlook that lies at the basis of Hegel's dialectical method is replaced by a new *philosophical outlook* that is no longer 'idealist' but 'materialist'. He seems to be unaware that *such* a 'materialist inversion' of Hegel's idealist philosophy involves at the most a merely terminological change whereby the Absolute instead of being called 'Spirit' is called 'Matter'. There is, however, an even more serious vice in Lenin's materialism. For he is not only annuls Marx and Engels's materialist inversion of the Hegelian dialectic; *he drags the whole debate between materialism and idealism back to a historical stage which German idealism from Kant to Hegel had already surpassed.* The dissolution of the metaphysical systems of Leibniz and Wolff began with Kant's transcendental philosophy and ended with Hegel's dialectic. Thereafter the 'Absolute' was definitively excluded from the *being* of both '*spirit*' and '*matter*', and was transferred into the dialectical *movement* of the '*idea*'. The materialist inversion by Marx and Engels of Hegel's idealist dialectic merely consisted in freeing this dialectic from its final mystifying shell. The *real movement of history* was discovered beneath the dialectical 'self-movement of the idea', and this revolutionary movement of history was proclaimed to be the only 'Absolute' remaining.[28] Lenin, however, goes back to the absolute polarities of

28. Cf. the famous passage in the afterword to the second edition of Marx's *Capital* in 1873 and also Engels's appreciation in the opening paragraphs of *Ludwig Feuerbach* of the 'true meaning and revolutionary character' of what he considers to be 'the conclusion of the whole movement from Kant' in Hegel's philosophy: 'The conservatism of this approach is relative, its revolutionary character is absolute – *the one absolute whose validity it permits.*' It would not be necessary to emphasize that the word '*absolute*', in Engels's text and my own, has only a figurative meaning if Lenin and those like him had not suddenly started once again to talk quite blandly and in a totally unfigurative way about absolute Being and absolute Truth.

'thought' and 'being', 'spirit' and 'matter', which had formed the basis of the philosophical, and even some of the religious, disputes that had divided the two currents of the Enlightenment in the seventeenth and eighteenth centuries.[29] Hegel, of course, had already surpassed these dialectically.

This kind of materialism is derived from a metaphysical idea of Being that is absolute and given; and despite all its formal claims to the contrary it is no longer fully dialectical let alone dialectically materialist. Lenin and his followers unilaterally transfer the dialectic into Object, Nature and History and they present knowledge merely as the passive mirror and reflection of this objective Being in the subjective Consciousness. In so doing they destroy both the dialectical interrelation of *being* and *consciousness* and, as a necessary consequence, the dialectical interrelation of *theory* and *prac-*

29. Cf. what is, despite all its inevitable mystification, an excellent historical critique by Hegel of both these trends within the Enlightenment philosophy of the seventeenth and eighteenth centuries in the *Phenomenology of the Spirit* (Baillie translation, pp. 592–3): 'The one kind of Enlightenment calls absolute Being that predicate-less Absolute, which exists in thought beyond the actual consciousness from which this Enlightenment started; the other calls it matter. If they were distinguished as Nature and Spirit or God, the unconscious inner working and weaving would have nothing of the wealth of developed life needed in order to be Nature, while Spirit or God would have no self-distinguishing consciousness. Both, as we saw, are entirely the same notion; the distinction lies not in the objective fact, but purely in the diversity of starting-point adopted by the two developments of thought, and in the fact that each stops at its own special point in the thought-process. If they rose above that, their thoughts would coincide, and they would find out that what is to the one, as it professes, a horror, and is to the other, a folly are one and the same thing.' Cf. on this Marx's materialist critique in the *Holy Family*, not of Hegel's presentation of materialism and theism as 'two sides of the same basic principle', but of the diluted substance which Bruno Bauer extracts from it.

tice. They thereby manage to pay an involuntary tribute to the 'Kantianism' that they attack so much. Not content with this, they have abandoned the question of the *relationship between the totality of historical being and all historically prevalent forms of consciousness*. This was first posed by Hegel's dialectic and was then given a more comprehensive elaboration by the dialectical materialism of Marx and Engels. Lenin and those like him have revised it in a retrograde way by replacing it with the much narrower epistemological or 'gnoseological' question of the *relationship between the subject and object of knowledge*. Nor is this all. They present knowledge as a fundamentally harmonious *evolutionary progress* and an *infinite progression towards absolute truth*. Their presentation of the relationship between theory and practice in general, and in particular within the revolutionary movement itself, is a complete abandonment of Marx's dialectical materialism and a retreat to a totally abstract opposition of pure *theory*, which discovers truths, to pure *practice*, which applies these laboriously discovered truths to reality. 'The real unity of theory and practice is achieved by changing reality in practice, through the revolutionary movement based on the laws of objective development discovered by theory' – these are the words of one of Lenin's philosophical interpreters, and he has not departed one iota from the teachings of the master. With them, the grandiose dialectical materialist unity of Marx's revolutionary practice collapses into a *dualism* comparable to that of the most typical bourgeois *idealists*.[30]

30. Cf. both Marx's 1845 *Theses on Feuerbach* and A. Deborin's account of the 'dialectical relationship of revolutionary theory to practice in his critical text on 'Lukács and his Critique of Marxism' *Arbeiter-literatur*, p. 640). There is no need here to provide specific examples of all the ways in which Lenin reduces Marxist theory to an undialectical

There is another inevitable consequence of this displacement of the accent from the *dialectic* to *materialism*. It prevents materialist philosophy from contributing to the further development of the empirical sciences of nature and society. In the dialectic *method and content are inseparably linked*: in a famous passage Marx says that 'form has no value when it is not the form of its content'.[31] It is therefore completely against the spirit of the dialectic, and especially of the materialist dialectic, to *counterpose* the dialectical materialist 'method' to the substantive results achieved by applying it to philosophy and the sciences. This procedure has become very fashionable in Western Marxism. Nevertheless, behind this exaggeration there lies a correct insight – namely, that dialectical materialism influenced the progress of the empirical study of nature and society in the second half of the nineteenth century above all because of its method.[32]

---

conception, since his position is explicitly stated on every page of his philosophical work. It need only be mentioned that throughout his work, which pursues the relations of Being and consciousness across nearly four hundred pages, Lenin always deals with these relations from an abstract epistemological standpoint. He never analyses knowledge on the same plane as other socio-historic forms of consciousness, and he never examines it as a historical phenomenon, as the idoelogical 'superstructure' of the economic structure of society at any given time (see Marx's Preface to the *Critique of Political Economy*) or even merely as the '*general expression of the real relations of existing class struggles*' (*Communist Manifesto*).

31. See Mehring's *Nachlassausgabe*, I, p. 319.

32. This was sometimes acknowledged by the Russian theorist Plekhanov, Lenin's philosophical teacher, and a man who for a definite period of history was regarded by Orthodox Marxists in East and West as the only authority on philosophical issues related to Marxism. For example, in the 1913 German edition of his *Basic Problems of Marxism*, there is the following statement in which he passes from an exposition of materialist philosophy to a discussion of the dialectical materialist method and its application to the sciences of nature and society: 'The materialist conception of history has first of all [*sic*] a *methodological*

When the revolutionary movement and its practice came to a halt in the 1850s, there inevitably developed an *increasing gap between the evolution of philosophy and that of the positive sciences, between the evolution of theory and that of practice*: this has already been explained in *Marxism and Philisophy*. The result was that for a long period the new revolutionary con-

---

significance.' The philosophical relation of Lenin to Plekhanov is such that it is the pupil who, after blindly adopting all the master's fundamental teachings, then goes on without hesitation to take them to their logical conclusions. Later on Plekhanov together with his pupil Axelrod made an orthodox 'revision' of his philosophical views 'in the sense of getting somewhat nearer to Kantian philosophy'. But it is historically false not only for Bolsheviks but also for left Mensheviks like Schifrin to describe this evolution as a result of the political 'deviation to social-patriotism' which they both committed during the war. (See the critical study on 'Soviet Marxism' mentioned above, p. 120 and note 17.) The truth of the matter is that much earlier, especially in the first (1902) and second (1905) editions of his translation of Engels's *Ludwig Feuerbach*, Plekhanov came far nearer than Lenin ever did to the theory of epistemology held by some modern natural scientists and which was tinged with Kantianism. See for this the two versions of Plekhanov's 'theory of hieroglyphics' cited in note 82 of Lenin's *Materialism and Empirio-Criticism* (*Collected Works*, vol. 14, p. 378). The author of this note, L. Rudas, slavishly repeats the position which Lenin had previously adopted for tactical reasons and he describes the *second* of these two formulations as still being a 'correction' of the first 'erroneous' one. However, a scientific comparison of these two formulations shows that in the Leninist sense of the word Plekhanov is equally 'agnostic' on both occasions; in 1903 he claims that things in themselves have 'no form' apart from their effects on us, and in 1920 he characterizes our sensations as 'a kind of hieroglyphics' that do not resemble occurrences but which 'quite correctly reproduce both occurrences themselves and – most importantly – the relations that exist between them'. The one advantage of the later over the earlier version is that it 'makes no terminological concessions to its philosophical opponents' and so the new version does not exhibit so bluntly the complete misinterpretation of the epistemological problematic that lies at the basis of the whole theory of hieroglyphics. I have discussed this in more detail in my *Auseinandersetzung mit Kautsky*, pp. 111ff.

ceptions of Marx and Engels survived and developed mainly through their application as a dialectical materialist method to the empirical sciences of society and nature. It is in this period that one finds statements, especially by the later Engels, formally proclaiming individual sciences to be independent of 'all philosophy', and asserting that philosophy has been 'driven from nature and from history' into the only field of activity left to it: 'the theory of thought and its laws – formal logic and dialectics'. In reality, this meant that Engels reduced so-called 'philosophy' from an individual science *above* others, to an empirical science *among* others.[33] Lenin's later positions might appear at first glance to be like that of Engels, but they are in actual fact as distinct as night and day. Engels considered that it was the crucial task of the materialist dialectic to 'rescue the *conscious dialectic* from German idealism and to incorporate it in the materialist conception of nature and of history'.[34] Lenin's procedure is the inverse. For him the major task is to uphold and defend the *materialist position* which no one has ever seriously thought of questioning. Engels goes on to make a statement that is in keeping with the progress and development of the sciences; he says that modern materialism whether applied to nature or history 'is in both cases essentially dialectical and does not in addition need a philosophy

33. See in particular the last section of *Ludwig Feuerbach and the End of Classical German Philosophy*, where Engels states explicitly that his and Marx's dialectical materialist viewpoint 'renders all philosophy both unnecessary and impossible', in both *history* and *nature*. See also the general statements in the introduction to *Anti-Dühring*, where he states that 'any particular science of the general totality is unnecessary' for modern 'essentially dialectical' materialism which assigns every particular branch of knowledge the task of making clear its own place in the whole system of things and of the knowledge of things.

34. Foreword to the second (1885) edition of *Anti-Dühring*.

which stands above the other branches of knowledge'. Lenin, however, insistently carps at 'philosophical deviations' that he has discerned not only among political friends or enemies, or philosophical ideologues, but even among the most creative natural scientists.[35] His 'materialist philosophy' becomes a kind of supreme judicial authority for evaluating the findings of individual sciences, past, present or future.[36] This material-

35. See, as one example among many, Lenin's peculiar 'philosophical' commentary on Helmholtz's *Handbuch der physiologischen Optik* in which on one and the same page sensations are described as '*symbols* of the relations of the external world without any similarity or likeness to what they describe' and then as '*effects* of the observed or represented object on our nervous system and on our consciousness'. Lenin says of the first statement '*This is agnosticism!*' and of the second '*This is materialism!*' He does not realize that there is no contradiction between these two statements of Helmholtz's, since an 'effect' does not need to have any similarity or likeness with its cause. The alleged 'inconsistency' in this natural scientist's representation has been introduced by the 'philosophical' critic; what he wants is not science but only a 'consistent' avowal of one or other metaphysical position (*Collected Works*, vol. 14, pp. 232ff.).

36. Lenin, in applying his judicial procedure, has an uncritical approach to the natural-scientific materialism of the second half of the nineteenth century which is highly abstract and without the slightest trace of a dialectic; it is not even openly stated. An example of this uncritical approach and of the enormous difference in this respect between Lenin's narrow 'philosophical' application of materialism and concrete historical materialism can be found by comparing the final section of Lenin's work on 'Ernst Haeckel and Ernst Mach' (op. cit., pp. 346–56) with the critical appreciation of Haeckel's *Welträtsel* (*Riddle of the Universe*) by the German left radical Franz Mehring, *Neue Zeit*, XVIII, I, pp. 417ff. Lenin's work adopts a totally inadequate materialist standpoint and this is strikingly indicated by the sentence of Mehring's Lenin himself cites (op. cit., p. 355): 'Haeckel's work, both in its less good and its very good aspects, is eminently adapted to help clarify the apparently rather confused views prevailing in the party as to the significance for it of *historical* materialism, on the one hand, and historical *materialism*, on the other.' There is another equally telling

ist 'philosophical' domination covers all the sciences, whether of nature or society, as well as all other cultural developments in literature, drama, plastic arts and so on; and Lenin's epigones have taken it to the most absurd lengths. This has resulted in a specific kind of *ideological dictatorship* which oscillates between revolutionary progress and the blackest reaction. Under the slogan of what is called 'Marxism-Leninism', this dictatorship is applied in Russia today to the whole intellectual life not only of the ruling Party, but of the working-class in general. There are now attempts to extend it from Russia to all the Communist Parties in the West, and in the rest of the world. These attempts, however, have precisely shown the inevitable limits to any such artificial extension of this ideological dictatorship into the international arena outside Russia, where it no longer receives the direct coercive support of the State. The Draft Programme of the Communist International, of the Fifth Comintern Congress of 1924, called for a 'rigorous struggle against idealist philosophy and against all philosophies other than dialectical materialism', whereas at the Sixth Congress, held four years later, the version of the Programme that was finally adopted spoke in a

---

passage which goes: 'Whoever wants to grasp for themselves how this limited natural-scientific materialism is incapable of coping with social matters; whoever wants to realize how fully natural-scientific materialism must develop into historical materialism, if it is really to become an irresistible analytic weapon in the great struggle for human liberation, must read Haeckel's book' (Mehring, op. cit., pp. 418, 419). In this connection one might compare the telling criticism which Engels made in the manuscripts of the *Dialectics of Nature* against Haeckel, the materialist scientist, with both Mehring and Lenin who regard him in a positive light (*Marx-Engels Archiv*, II, especially pp. 117, 234 ('Promammale Haeckel'!), 259 and 260). Lenin talks quite positively of the famous scientist Haeckel (without quotation marks) in contrast to the 'famous philosopher Mach' (with quotation marks) and of Haeckel's 'all-powerful materialism'.

much more general way of the struggle against 'all manifestations of a bourgeois outlook'. It no longer described 'the dialectical materialism of Marx and Engels' as a materialist philosophy, but only as a 'revolutionary method(!) for understanding reality with the aim of its revolutionary overthrow'.[37]

IV

It is only recently that 'Marxist-Leninist' ideology has made such claims outside Russia, and the change in Comintern policy I have mentioned may indicate that these claims are now going to be abandoned. Nevertheless, the deeper problem of Lenin's 'materialist philosophy' and of Marxism-Leninism has not been resolved. The problem of *Marxism and Philosophy* must be reopened, together with the broader issue of the *relation between the ideology and the practice of the revolutionary workers' movement*. This poses a concrete task in relation to Communist 'Marxism-Leninism'. A materialist, that is a historical, critical and undogmatic analysis has already been made of the character of the 'Kautskyian' orthodox Marxism of the Second International. This must now be unflinchingly extended to the 'Leninist' orthodox Marxism of the Third International; and it must be applied to the whole history of Russian Marxism and its relation to international Marxism. For the 'Marxism-Leninism' of today is only the latest offshoot of this history. It is not possible to provide

37. On the different versions of the programme see *Internationale Pressekorrespondenz* (in German), 1924, no. 136, p. 1796, and *Inprecorr*, 1928, no. 92, p. 1750; see also Bukharin's speeches on the programme at the Fifth and Sixth Congresses of the Communist International, in *Fifth Congress of the Communist International*, published by the Comminist Party of Great Britain, pp. 131ff., and *Inprecorr*, 1928, no. 59, p. 1034.

a more concrete elaboration here. One can only indicate a very general outline of such a materialist account of the real history of Marxism in Russia and elsewhere. Even so it yields a sobering conclusion. Russian Marxism, which was if possible *even more 'orthodox'* than German Marxism, had throughout its history an *even more ideological character* and if possible was in *even greater conflict* with the concrete historical movement of which it was the ideology.

Trotsky's perceptive critical analysis of 1908 showed that this was true of the *first phase of its history*. The Russian intelligentsia had previously been brought up in the Bakuninist 'spirit of a simple rejection of capitalist culture', and Marxism served as an ideological instrument to reconcile them to the development of capitalism.[38] It is also valid for the *second phase*, which reached its climax in the first Russian Revolution of 1905. At that time all revolutionary Marxists in Russia, not least Lenin and Trotsky, declared themselves to be part of 'the flesh and blood' of international socialism – and for them this meant *orthodox Marxism*. On the other side Karl Kautsky and his *Neue Zeit* were in complete agreement with orthodox Russian Marxism on all theoretical questions. Indeed, as far as the philosophical foundations of its theory were concerned, German orthodox Marxism was more influenced by Russian Marxism than itself influential on it, since the Germans were to a considerable extent under the sway of

38. See Trotsky's article on the 25th Anniversary of *Neue Zeit*, *Neue Zeit*, XXVI, I, pp. 7ff. Further striking proofs of the contradictory evolutions of Marxist ideology and of the real movement in Russia, in both its early and subsequent phases of development are to be found in Schifrin, 'On the Genesis of Socio-Economic Ideologies in Russian Economics' (*Archiv für Sozialwissenschaft und Sozialpolitik*, vol. 55, pp. 720ff.) and in the outstanding introduction by the editor Kurt Mandelbaum to the German edition of Marx and Engels's *Letters to Nikolaion* (Leipzig, 1929), pp. v–xxxiv.

the Russian theoretician Plekhanov. Thus a great international united front of Marxist orthodoxy was able to sustain itself without major difficulty, because historically it was only necessary for it to exist *in the realm of ideology* and *as ideology*. This was true both in the West and in Russia, and in Russia even more than in Central and Western Europe. Russian Marxism is now in its *third phase* and it still exhibits the same ideological character and the same inevitable concomitant contradiction between a professed 'orthodox' theory and the real historical character of the movement. It found its most vivid expression in Lenin's orthodox Marxist theory and his totally unorthodox practice;[39] and it is now caricatured by the glaring contradictions between theory and practice in contemporary 'Soviet Marxism'.

This general character of Russian Marxism has persisted without fundamental change into the 'Soviet Marxism' of today. Involuntary confirmation of this is provided by the position of the above-mentioned Schifrin, a political opponent of the ruling Bolshevik Party, on the general philosophical principles of Soviet Marxism. In an article in *Die Gesellschaft* (IV, 7), he made what looked like a fierce attack on 'Soviet Marxism', but from a philosophical point of view this really concealed a *defence* of it. He claims that Soviet Marxism 'wants to make a sincere attempt to reinforce Marxism in its most consistent and orthodox form' against degenerate 'subjectivist' and 'revisionist' tendencies (e.g. 'neglect of the master's most important statements'), that have emerged as a result of the insuperable difficulties that it is facing. The same bias is even clearer in another article of Schifrin in *Die Gesellschaft* of August 1929. In this, Schifrin discusses the

39. Cf. my article 'Lenin and the Comintern' mentioned above, note 15.

latest work by Karl Kautsky, the leading representative of German orthodox Marxism, and although he is very critical of most of Kautsky's individual positions, he greets Kautsky's book warmly as the beginning of a 'restoration of genuine Marxism'. He assigns Kautsky the 'ideological mission' of overcoming the various kinds of 'subjectivist disintegration of Marxism' that have recently appeared in the West as well as in 'Sovietized Russian Marxism', and of overcoming the 'ideological crisis' that this has caused throughout Marxism.[40] The article is particularly clear evidence of the *philosophical solidarity of the whole orthodox Marxist movement* down to this day. In his critique of contemporary Soviet Marxist 'Leninism' and in his attitudes to contemporary 'Kautsky-ism', Schifrin completely fails to see that both of these ideological versions of orthodox Marxism have emerged from the traditions of earlier Russian and international Marxism. *Today they only represent evanescent historical forms that date from a previous phase of the workers' movement.* Here, in this assessment of the character of 'Marxism-Leninism' and of 'Soviet Marxism', one can see the full and fundamental unity of outlook between the old and the new schools of contemporary orthodox Marxism: Social Democracy and Communism. It has been seen how Communist theoreticians reacted to *Marxism and Philosophy* by defending the positive and progressive character of the Marxism of the Second International. Now, in the periodical of German Social Democracy, one can see a Menshevik theoretician entering the lists to defend the 'generally valid' and 'compelling' philosophical features of the Marxism of the Third International.

This ends my account of the present state of the problem of *Marxism and Philosophy* – a problem that since 1923 has been

40. op. cit., pp. 149ff. Schifrin's italics.

changed in many ways by new theoretical and practical developments. The general outlines of my evolution since then are clear enough, and I have therefore refrained from correcting all the details of what I then said in the light of my present position. In only one respect does it appear to be necessary to make an exception. *Marxism and Philosophy* argued that during the social revolution a 'dictatorship' was necessary not only in the field of politics, but also that of ideology. This led to many misunderstandings, especially in the case of Kautsky. In his review of my book he showed both that he had misinterpreted my positions and that he had certain illusions about the conditions prevailing in Russia. Thus as late as 1924 he stated that 'dictatorship in the realm of ideas' had 'never occurred to anyone, not even to Zinoviev and Dzherzhinsky'. I now think that the abstract formulation of this demand in my book is genuinely misleading, and I must emphasize that the pursuit of revolutionary struggle by what *Marxism and Philosophy* called an 'ideological dictatorship' is in three respects different from the *system of intellectual oppression* established in Russia today in the name of the 'dictatorship of the proletariat'. First of all, it is a dictatorship *of* the proletariat and not *over* the proletariat. Secondly, it is a dictatorship of a class and not of a party or party leadership. Thirdly, and most importantly, as a revolutionary dictatorship it is one element only of that radical process of social overthrow which by suppressing classes and class contradictions creates the preconditions for a 'withering away of the State', and thereby the end of all ideological constraint. The essential purpose of an 'ideological dictatorship' in this sense is to abolish its own material and ideological causes and thereby to make its own existence unnecessary and impossible. *From the very first day*, this genuine proletarian dictatorship will be distinguished from every false imitation of it by its creation of the conditions of intellectual freedom not only for 'all' workers but for 'each individual' worker. Despite the alleged 'democracy' and 'freedom of thought' in bourgeois society, this freedom has never been enjoyed anywhere by the wage slaves who suffer its physical and spiritual oppression. This is what concretely defines the Marxist concept of the revolutionary *dictatorship of the proletariat.* With it disappears the otherwise apparent contradiction between a call for 'ideological dictatorship', and the essentially critical and revolutionary nature of the method and the outlook of Communism. *Socialism, both in its ends and in its means, is a struggle to realize freedom.*

Introduction to the Critique of the Gotha Programme [1922]

1. *The Outward History of the Letter on the Gotha Programme*

Next to the *Communist Manifesto* of 1847–8 and the 'General Introduction' to the *Critique of Political Economy* of 1857, the *Critique of the Gotha Programme* of 1875 is, of all Karl Marx's shorter works, the most complete, lucid and forceful expression of the bases and consequences of his economic and social theory.[1] But for this very reason, like the two others, it is not among the master's most easily comprehensible works. One obvious reason for this is that it is not written as a unified presentation, but is made up of loosely assembled 'marginal notes'[2] on individual paragraphs of a draft programme that itself was not structured in a rigorously logical way. To

1. Marx wrote the critique of the draft Programme of the Gotha Congress before the Congress itself took place. It was written for his German friends (Bracke, Geib, Auer, Bebel and Wilhelm Liebknecht) and was not published until 1891, when at Engels's request it was printed in *Neue Zeit* as a contribution to the discussion then taking place on the 1891 Erfurt Programme. See Marx and Engels's letters in *Selected Works*, vol. II, pp. 15–17, 45–8. The full text is in ibid., pp. 18ff.

2. The original German title is *Randglossen zum Programm der deutschen Arbeiterpartei* ('Marginal Notes on the Programme of the German Workers' Party'). [Translator's note.]

understand the content even of specific sections, the reader must know certain things in advance if he is to be able to grasp the rich and profound contents of the work in full. He must know something about certain historical facts and their general context, and also the theoretical meaning of certain concepts within the Marxist system. Otherwise what may happen is what occurred to those to whom Marx originally sent his letter in 1875. They totally failed to understand the theoretical and practical importance of Marx's critique and consequently they were in no position to undertake any essential changes in the draft Programme on the basis of it. As a result, the definitive version of the Programme adopted by the Gotha Party Congress in the same month, May 1875, varied so little from the draft which Marx criticized that not one of his criticisms ceased to apply to it. The recipients of the letter did not even understand the minor points he made. This is shown, for example, by the fact that they even failed to cross out 'the regulation of prison labour', although Marx criticized it at the end of his text as a 'petty demand in a general worker's programme'. They did not even improve it in the way Marx suggested. Yet this, as Marx justly commented, was 'the least one might have expected from socialists'. This demand remained in the Programme as one of the 'eight' immediate demands of the united German working class, which is really as if a newly founded revolutionary party had called for the 'abolition of the dog tax'. Marx's letter met with little real understanding among even the best representatives of Marxism in Germany itself, and anyone who wants to get a clearer idea of this need only read the lengthy account of the events surrounding the Programme given by August Bebel in his memoirs.[3] Bebel's self-satisfied conclusion is as

3. August Bebel, *My Life* (London, 1912), p. 287.

follows; 'One can see that it was no easy thing to reach agreement with the two old men [Marx and Engels] in London. What on our part was a clever calculation and an adroit tactic was seen by them as weakness and irresponsible complacency. In the end the main point was achieved: the unification. This logically contained within itself its own further development. As before and afterwards, those friends of ours, our enemies, made sure this was so.' The only thing right about these comforting reflections of the old party leader is in the last sentence; as had happened so often before in the history of the socialist movement, it was the enemies of socialism who did all they could to make up for the lack of principle of its friends. In the end this historical compensation reconciled even Marx and Engels, to some extent, with this 'extremely disorganized, confused, fragmented, illogical and disreputable Programme'. This is stated explicitly in a final 'Letter on the Programme' written on 12 October 1875 by Engels to August Bebel, in his and Marx's name.[4] In this letter Engels begins by restating the theoretical condemnation he and Marx had already expressed. The Programme would have doubtless made a 'laughing stock' of the party if there 'had been a single critical mind in the bourgeois press' able to point out the 'contradictions and economic howlers' it contained. Engels goes on to say that 'instead of this, the donkeys of the bourgeois papers took this programme quite seriously and read into it what it does not contain. They interpreted it in a communist way, and the workers appear to be doing the same. It is *this circumstance alone* that made it possible for Marx and myself not to dis-

4. *Selected Correspondence*, p. 363. Engels's letter to Bebel of 18–28 March 1875, in *Selected Works*, vol. 2, pp. 38ff., sets out in a more accessible form than Marx's *Critique* (which was written two months later) the most important critical objections of the two 'old men' to the Draft Programme.

sociate ourselves publicly from such a programme. As long as our opponents, and likewise the workers, view the programme as embodying our intentions we may allow ourselves to keep quiet about it.'

This is how Marx's critique of the Programme drafted for Gotha became, unwittingly, a critique of the Programme adopted in Gotha. Hence the reader who wants to get a general view of the object of Marx's criticism in order to understand Marx's notes can do this just as well by reading the finally adopted version of the Programme as by reading the preliminary draft Programme criticized by Marx himself. The two have exactly the same substantive content, and wherever there is a reference to the words of the draft, Marx himself quotes them in the *Critique*.

2. *The Revival of the Workers' Movement, 1849–75*

In the 1860s, after a long period in which the workers' movement of emancipation of 1848–9 had first been bloodily suppressed and then lulled, there were at last signs of a 're-awakening of the working classes in the most industrialized countries of Europe'. As a result the International Workingmen's Association (the First International) was founded in London on 28 September 1864 with Karl Marx as a leading participant; it lasted till 1874–6. In the *Inaugural Address* Marx prepared for the founding of the I.W.A. there is the following picture, concise and rich, of the general character of the 'post-revolutionary' epoch between 1848 and the formation of the First International.

After the failure of the revolutions of 1848, all party organizations and party journals of the working class were, on the continent, crushed by the iron hand of force, the most advanced sons of labour fled in despair to the Transatlantic Republic, and the short-lived dreams of emancipation vanished before an epoch of industrial fever, moral degeneration and political reaction. The defeat of the continental working classes, owing partly to the diplomacy of the English government, then as now in fraternal solidarity with the cabinet of St Petersburg, soon spread its contagious effects to this side of the channel. While the rout of their continental brethren unmanned the English working classes, and broke their faith in their own cause, it restored to the landlord and the capitalist their somewhat shaken confidence. They insolently withdrew concessions already advertised. The discoveries of new goldlands led to an immense exodus, leaving an irrevocable void in the ranks of the British proletariat. Others of its formerly active members were caught by the temporary bribe of greater work and wages, and turned into loyal workers. All the efforts made to sustain or remodel the Chartist Movement failed quite unambiguously. The press organs of the working class died one by one of the apathy of the masses, and, in point of fact, never before did the English working class seem so thoroughly reconciled to a state of political nullity. If, then, there had been no solidarity of action between the British and continental working classes, there was, at all events, a solidarity of defeat.

When, after such a period of defeat, the first hopes were aroused once again, Marx and Engels eagerly seized the first occasion 'to do significantly practical and theoretical work' once again on a wider scale within the movement of proletarian emancipation. Nevertheless they were clear that it was not yet possible at this stage to use the 'old audacity of language' employed in the *Communist Manifesto* of 1847–8. The task was rather to have a position which was resolute, substantive and did not compromise on any question of principle, but to make it *politically effective* in a form that was broad and cautious, and did not exclude any sympathetic collaborators. With this in mind Marx wrote the *Inaugural Address* and the Provisional Statutes of the I.W.A. which were later adopted by the Geneva Congress in 1866 with few alterations.[5] The reader will see that, apart from the vacuous final section which Marx only added reluctantly and under the pressure of necessity, this declaration of principles expressed in substance the basic ideas and conclusions of communism just as accurately as the verbally much more passionate and stormy *Manifesto of the Communist League*.

As for the decade between 1864 and 1874, Marx and Engels reckoned that the working masses of Europe had acquired a greater 'awareness of the real preconditions of emancipating the workers'. Engels gave the following picture of the importance of this period in his 1890 preface to the *Communist Manifesto*:

When the working class of Europe had again gathered sufficient strength for a new onslaught upon the power of the ruling classes, the International Workingmen's Association came into being. Its aim was to weld together into *one* huge army the whole militant working class of Europe and America. Therefore it could not *set out* from the principles laid down in the Manifesto. It was bound to have a programme which would not shut the door on the English trade unions, the French, Belgian, Italian and Spanish Proudhonists and the German Lassalleans. This programme – the preamble to the Statutes of the International – was drawn up by Marx with a master hand, acknowledged even by Bakunin and the anarchists. For the ultimate triumph of the ideas set forth in the Manifesto, Marx relied solely and exclusively upon the intellectual development of the working class, as it necessarily had to ensue from united action and discussion. The events and vicissitudes in the struggle against capital, the defeats even more than the successes, could not but demonstrate to the fighters the inadequacy hitherto of their universal panaceas and make their minds more receptive to a thorough understanding of the true conditions for the emancipation of the workers. And Marx was right. The working class of 1874, at the dissolution of the International, was altogether different from that of 1864, at its foundation. Proudhonism in the Latin countries and Lassalleanism in Germany were dying out, and even the arch-conservative

5. *Selected Works*, vol. 1, pp. 377ff.

English trade unions were gradually approaching the point where in 1887 the chairman of their Swansea Congress could say in their name: 'Continental Socialism has lost its terrors for us.' Yet by 1887 Continental Socialism was almost exclusively the theory heralded in the Manifesto.[6]

In the middle of the 1870s, then, Marx and Engels thought it was far more possible than they had ten years earlier for the socialist and communist movement in the advanced countries to return to the 'old audacity' of the 1847–8 *Manifesto* by exhibiting a 'declaration of principles'. In any case, they thought that the movement had developed to an extent that any *retreat* from what was said in 1864 must appear to be an unforgivable crime against the future of the workers' movement. Thus Marx himself says in the note accompanying his *Critique of the Gotha Programme*:[7] there was no need to make a 'declaration of principles' when conditions did not allow it, but when conditions had progressed so much since 1864, it was utterly impermissible to 'demoralize' the party with a shallow and unprincipled programme.

This illustrates some of Marx's preoccupations when writing the *Critique of the Gotha Programme*. He demanded from the 'Declaration of Principles' of the most advanced Socialist Democratic party *as a minimum* the same level of principle and concrete demands as he himself had been able to insert into another declaration of principles, ten years earlier. This had been drafted under much less favourable circumstances and was designed for the common programme of the various socialist, half-socialist and quarter-socialist tendencies in Europe and America. Wherever the Gotha Programme failed to meet this minimum condition, Marx considers it to have

6. *Selected Works*, vol. I, pp. 30–1.

7. Letter to Bracke, *Selected Works*, vol. II, p. 16.

fallen below the level already reached by the movement. Hence, even if it appeared to suit the state of the Party in Germany, it was bound to harm the future historical development of the movement.

3. *Marx and Lassalle*

One can acquire a deeper understanding of the basic propositions of the *Critique* by looking into the historical and intellectual relations and conflicts between those two world-historical personalities, Marx and Lassalle. The reader must learn to see Marx's letter in terms of the great dispute between Lassalle and Marx, i.e. between an already *developed* and philosophically idealist German socialism and an international Marxist communism that was still in the initial process of *developing* on a far mightier scale. It was the circumstances surrounding the Gotha Unification Congress that served as the external reason for Marx's conviction that it was necessary to have such a dispute at this time. We know that at Gotha the former Lassalleans (the *Allgemeine Deutsche Arbeiterverein*) and the former Eisenachers (the *Sozialistische Arbeiterpartei Deutschlands*) came together to form the unified *Sozialistische Arbeiterpartei Deutschlands*. Up to then, the Eisenacher tendency appeared to be the Marxist one, owing to historical and partly personal and contingent factors which one can study in Mehring's biography of Marx or in his history of German Social Democracy. At the same time it must be rather surprising to see how partisanly Marx in his *Critique of the Gotha Programme* attributes every single defect and mistake in the unified German Party's programme to the 'Lassalleanist' tendency. This is especially surprising if one recalls his tolerance and patience towards the totally uncommunist principles of many sections of the International Workingmen's Association, which he formed and led. Lassalle, moreover, had been dead for more than a decade. He had not even been alive when the I.W.A. was set up in 1864. Also, it is evident from their theoretical writings and by their practical positions on many questions, and emerges particularly clearly from Mehring's neutral account, that the Lassalleaner were in many ways better 'Marxists' than the Eisenacher. In some of its formulations of principle, the Eisenach Programme of 1869 had formally followed the International's Statutes but in others it followed 'Lassallean' principles as much as the Gotha Programme itself. Marx appears to go too far in his criticism of the corrupting and demoralizing influence of Lassalleanism in the draft Programme. To gain a full understanding of the real meaning and of the theoretical and historical justification for this, one must go deeper and realize that Marx was a thinker and politician who was highly conscious of his historical responsibilities and was 'working for the world'. In dealing with the draft Programme he was not backing the 'Eisenach' tendency in German Social Democracy against the 'Lassalleans'. Rather, he was trying to fight and demolish the *Lassallean spirit* which was much more influential than the Marxist spirit among both the Eisenachers and the Lassalleaner. Karl Marx wrote the greater part of his letter against the 'living Lassalle'. He was trying, retrospectively and definitively, to demolish Lassalle's conception of society, which was based on a philosophy of Right and of the State, and therefore on 'idealism'. His aim is to replace it, theoretically and practically, with the 'materialist' conception of history founded on the economy. This was the outlook which for over thirty years, in alliance with the few who really understood him, he had struggled and laboured to advance. One can say that from 1843 (when he attained his decisive 'materialist' outlook in the *Critique of Hegel's Philosophy of Right*) all Marx's writings and actions were fundamentally contributions to the advance of this materialist outlook and practice, against the ever-growing army of its opponents both within and without the walls of the proletarian camp. We know only too well now that this struggle is as necessary today as it was fifty or eighty years ago. The irony of history has willed it that the numerically strongest socialist tendency in Germany, the German Social Democratic Party (SPD), has just formally abandoned Marxism, in its new Görlitz Programme of 23 September 1921. In its place the SPD has once again written on its banners the slogans of Lassalle which Marx tried to annihilate in his critique of the Gotha Programme. Of course, all it has repeated are the *words* of Lassalle, since the German Social Democratic Party of 1921, which rejects Marxism, has as little to do with the *spirit* of Lassalle as with that of Marx. In Lassalle's great speech of 1862 (what is called the 'Workers' Programme') *On the Especial Connection of the Present Historical Period with the Idea of the Working Class* there are many formulations which conflict with the Görlitz Programme of 1921. Among these is the clear statement that 'the period of history which began in spring 1848 will not produce a state, whether of a monarchic or republican form, which expresses or maintains the political domination of the Third Estate'. At the same time, the reference to Lassalle by the defenders of the Görlitz Programme still has a certain significance. If we said this was 1862 and not 1923, we might still regard this programme of a 'party of the working people' as a product of Lassallean doctrine. In one and the same breath, it describes the class struggle to liberate the proletariat as a 'historical necessity' and as an 'ethical demand'; and it declares its intention to struggle for 'the popular will organized in a free people's state' to dominate the economy and society. Such a programme could only properly be called Lassallean, however, if something very different were said 'in private'. For everything Lassalle ever wrote or said about 'universal suffrage' and related matters is put in a totally different light by what he once said, in true bourgeois style, to a close circle of confidants. 'Whenever I say "universal suffrage" you must understand me to mean "revolution", and only "revolution".' However true this may be, we do not, unfortunately, have among us the 'living Lassalle' to contradict the 'dead' Braun, Cunow, Kampffmeyer and their companions. Lassalle's revolutionary slogans of 1862 have been criminally misused to justify and embellish a completely non-revolutionary and anti-revolutionary, petty bourgeois and utterly hopeless programme of utopian reform. Lassalle only survives in printed form and in literature, but he is far less able to combat these caricatures than another more powerful opponent of them who survives in the same form, Karl Marx.

4. *The Materialist and Ideological Conceptions of History*

The central target of all Marx's criticisms of the Gotha Programme is the Lassallean and Social Democratic conception of the State and of society, which is thoroughly ideological. At the time it was still held by most German Social Democrats and it was very clearly articulated in the draft Programme. This was a fateful time for the socialist movement. The most numerous socialist workers' party which the world has so far seen was coming into existence. For Marx it was once again necessary to protest – in an unequivocally vigorous way, as always, against opportunism – at a draft Programme which contained the characteristic ideological errors of Lassallean socialism, scientifically long outdated and now merely heated up again. In doing so, Marx had to affirm the validity in all its rigour and results of the basic 'materialist' principle of which he had summed up some decades before in the following pregnant passage: 'Legal relations as well as forms of the state are to be grasped neither from themselves nor from the so-called general development of the human mind, but rather have their roots in the material conditions of life, the sum total of which Hegel, following the example of the Englishmen and Frenchmen of the eighteenth century, combined under the name of "civil society". However, the anatomy of civil society is to be sought in political economy.'[8] In direct contradiction to this materialist and economic conception of Marx, the Gotha Programme in its very first sentence accepts the thoroughly ideological position of Lassalle, according to which the claim of all members of society to the product of their labour should be based on the idea of 'equal right'. Founded on this lofty principle, it proceeds consistently in section II to demand a 'free State' in which 'all social and political inequality' is overcome, and ends by making only one socio-economic demand – the establishment of producers' co-operatives 'with State aid'. The draft (and the definitive version of the Programme) add to this no less than seven purely political and bourgeois-democratic demands. According to Engels every one of these 'directly and literally coincides with the Programme of the People's Party and the petty bourgeois democracy'.[9] The one instance of 'internationalism' is an abstract, ideological-political profession of the idea of the 'international brotherhood of peoples' (changed in the final version to the 'brotherhood of men').

8. *Selected Works*, vol, I, p. 362.
9. *Selected Works*, vol, II, p. 39.

Karl Marx had devoted his whole life to transforming socialism from a theoretical ideology and practical utopia into a realistic and material science and practice. It is not surprising that a programme like this deeply disappointed and dismayed him. This is why the whole letter on the Programme became one blazing indictment of what he explicitly stated to be a 'thoroughly objectionable programme, which would demoralize the Party' in everything it said. The theory and practice of scientific socialism is materialist. The draft Programme is Lassallean – that is, ideological and utopia. Even if one were able and willing to ignore this, 'the Programme is worthless' taken in and for itself. Marx therefore holds it to be his 'duty' 'not to accept' such a theoretically and practically unprincipled Programme 'by a diplomatic silence'. He 'comments on' it and 'criticizes' it with the greatest thoroughness.

5. *The Dialectical Method*

The *form* in which Marx carried out his decision to criticize the Programme is extremely suggestive of his whole intellectual formation. It shows particularly clearly the enormous superiority of the 'materialist' method. Marx also applied this method to the production of theoretical ideas and it is often referred to as the 'dialectical' method, a formulation retained by Marx and Engels.[10] According to Marx's basic materialist conception, intellectual production like any other production requires a specific, concrete raw material to be transformed into thought. Thinking which just produces abstract thoughts

10. This is discussed in more detail in my forthcoming book, 'The Philosophical Foundations of Marxism' [Translator's note: i.e. *Marxism and Philosophy*].

'in general' is quite fruitless. Even in thinking, the only way to produce a real 'material' product of thought is by applying the power of thought to a material of thought which can be worked on by it. This means that Marx did not proceed to criticize the Gotha Programme by revealing the false and superficial general principle that clearly underlies all its particular sentences and demands, and then simply counterpose the truer and deeper principle of his materialism to it, in an equally general form. He proceeds inversely, by criticizing in the greatest detail each individual passage in the Programme. This is a highly skilful work of intellectual production. Its individual propositions might sometimes appear at first sight to be arbitrary or hair-splitting; but on closer inspection they always turn out to be important and necessary steps within the whole process of the argument. Marx takes what at first appear to be quite harmless passages from the draft, and extracts from them all the fundamental vagueness, the timid indecision, the wordy nullity and futility contained within them. This reveals most clearly, but in a *mediate* way, the abysmal falsity of the basic principle underlying all these passages. This means that the fundamental conflict between the Marxist-materialist and the Lassallean-ideological conceptions of history is never stated in a general form anywhere in the letter, although from the start it governs every particular statement in it. It runs like a red thread through all the specific 'marginal notes' binding them into a tight-knit unity, and is clearly visible everywhere to those familiar with it. Karl Marx was a *positive dialectician and revolutionary* and the magnificent character of his spirit is very evident in the *Critique*: he never allows his critical work to become a mere *negation* of the errors and superficialities analysed in his letter. He always goes on to expound or briefly indicate the *positive* and *true* concepts which should replace the error and illusion he criticizes. He is not content to criticize and refute the parts of the Programme which are the results of a false and superficial principle. This refutation always yields a positive development of conclusions drawn from the deeper and truer materialist position which he advances in its place. It is through this *positive* development that the process comes to an end in a way that the 'materialist dialectician' finds really satisfying.

6. *From Marx to Lenin*

It is, of course, these *positive developments* which are the most important and concretely significant parts of the *Critique* for the theory and practice of contemporary Marxism. For the *Critique* does not just contain a set of Marx's discoveries assembled in highly concise and compelling formulas, yet available elsewhere. We find here Marx's own systematic *application* of his basic materialist principle to a set of major social problems on which he nowhere else spoke with equal clarity and at such length. Above all, Marx here fundamentally clarifies the real theoretical and practical relationship between the present and future 'society' and the (present and future) 'State', in contradistinction to Lassalle's ideology of Right and of the State. There is no need to indicate how enormously important the Gotha Programme is in this respect today. The reader can find a critical evaluation and elaboration, in the finest Marxist spirit, of all the relevant passages from the *Critique of the Gotha Programme* in the fifth chapter of that classical work on the theory and practice of the Marxist conception of the State, Lenin's *State and Revolution*. In twenty highly concentrated pages, Lenin discusses the problem of the relationship of society and the State, and the related questions of the transition from capitalism to communism, the different forms of democracy and dictatorship, and their supersession by the gradual *emergence* of a future *communist society*. This communist society develops from capitalist society and will, for a long time, be defined and its 'free development' hindered by the latter's traditions and forms. All that Lenin said in this connection appears quite explicitly as a consistent development of the basic insights that Marx first developed on these issues in his letter on the Gotha Programme in 1875. Marx, at the height of his powers, wrote in sharp opposition to the Lassallean and German Social Democratic, ideological and utopian, conception of that *State*, which has predominated in the European and American workers' movement to this day. The practical politics of a real Marxist is only the continuation by other means of his theoretical work of science and propaganda.[11] Thus, in a certain sense, the whole great world-historical event of the proletarian revolution in Russia after 1917 is but a continuation into *practical reality* of the fundamental materialist principle of the development of history and society. It was the theoretical realization of this principle for which Marx fought and worked in all his writings, but most decisively of all in the *Critique of the Gotha Programme*.

7. *The Structure of the Letter*

Corresponding to the divisions in the draft Programme under criticism (which only differs from the final version in a few

11. To gain an emphatic appreciation of this, one should read the famous twelve-line postscript to *State and Revolution* which Lenin wrote in Petrograd on 30 November 1917, and which ends with this sentence: 'It is more pleasant and more useful to *live through* a revolution than to *write about* it.'

details), Marx's *Critique* falls into four sections, or, if one takes the initial formulations of the fourth section on the concept of the 'free state' as an independent part, five sections.[12] Section IV.B consists of the draft's *immediate political and cultural demands*. Marx's critique of these demands is extremely clear and thorough; it needs no elaboration here as it will be immediately comprehensible to the reader. A further study of this part of the Marxist-Communist critique of the Social Democratic Party's Programme would include, first of all, Engels's letter 'On the Critique of the Social Democratic Draft Programme of 1891 (the Erfurt Programme)', which was first published in *Neue Zeit* (1901) and in a certain sense continues the joint critique by Marx and Engels of the draft Gotha Programme.[13] What Marx and Engels would have said about the 1921 Görlitz Programme of the German Social Democrats can be left to the imagination of the reader, alerted by studying this text. Anyone who wants a more precise guidance can read the relevant writings of Rosa Luxemburg, Lenin, Trosky and Radek.

The section of the letter that is basic to all the others is the comprehensive *first section*. Under numbers 1 and 2 and with the short section II, it contains a highly concentrated account of Marxist *political economy*. Under number 3 and with section III it serves to prepare for the important statements of section IV of the relationship of *society* and the *State*, now and in the future. In our own time Lenin has developed these ideas in both theory and practice. Finally, under numbers 4 and 5, there are some very important remarks, particularly pertinent today, on the historical relationship of the proletariat to the other *classes* in the different phases of the development of

12. The numbering used here is that in *Selected Works*, vol. II. [Translator's note.]

13. *Selected Correspondence*, p. 512.

capitalist society, on the necessarily *international content* of the workers' movement, and above all on the international tasks of the German working class. These form a development of analyses in the *Communist Manifesto*.

Sections I and II of the *Critique* make an important though brief contribution to clarifying the basic concepts and theses of Marxist political economy, and it is naturally both impossible and unnecessary to discuss them once again in this short treatment. The reader who still has difficulty with these sections of the *Critique* is referred to my recently published *Quintessenz des Marxismus*. There he will find, in an extremely short and precise form, thirty-seven questions and answers which explain all the basic concepts and theories of Marxist economics as well as the most essential theses of the Marxist theory of society. Having done so, he will be ready to understand those parts of the *Critique* which are hard to comprehend without some knowledge of Marxist concepts and their place within the whole economic and social theory of Marxism. To this very day these are still catastrophically misunderstood even by good followers of Marx.

8. *Two Difficult Questions: The Iron Law of Wages and Producers' Co-operatives with State Aid*

Of all the difficult passages in the *Critique* that are liable to be misunderstood, there are only two that need some further discussion, in that I think that they are the most difficult ones for beginners. These are the statements in sections II and III on the so-called 'iron law of wages' and 'producers' co-operatives with State aid'. It is on these points that there has frequently been great misunderstanding of Marx's strong criticism of the Gotha Programme, and a tendency to see in it an 'excessive' expression of Marx's specifically personal animosity towards Lassalle. There can be no dispute about the personally bitter tone in which Marx and Engels attacked Lassalle at this time, but their expressions are the result of an ineluctable and concrete necessity. For it is precisely where the formulations and demands of materialist-communist Marxism and ideological-socialist Lassalleanism are externally so close that their inner contradiction is so much greater. To ignore this contradiction is very dangerous, if the scientific insights finally attained by Marx are to be preserved and developed.

We begin with the *law of wages*. First, let us mention Marx's critical remark in his letter that 'proceeds of labour' is a 'loose' (i.e. imprecise) idea which 'Lassalle has put in the place of definite economic concepts'. The 'definite economic concepts' Marx talks of here are obviously those of his theory of value and surplus value, and in particular a scientific discovery that is basic for any understanding of Marxist communism, but which is regarded today as 'meaningless' by all his opponents and even by some of his followers. This discovery is that *wages* are not, as the bourgeois economists would have it, the value (or price) *of labour* but only 'a masked form of the value or price of *labour power*', which is sold on the labour market as a commodity before it is employed productively (as labour) in the capitalist's enterprise. I have explained the theoretical basis of these concepts and phrases elsewhere, in my *Quintessenz des Marxismus*. But what is only discussed theoretically there can be seen applied in an immensely important and practical way in the *Critique* itself. It is not without justification, nor out of blind hostility to Lassalle and his followers, that Karl Marx lays such emphatic stress on these key aspects of his theory of surplus value and fights Lassalle's slogan 'the iron law of wages' with such merciless vigour. At first sight there would appear to be no real contradiction between what Marx and Lassalle say. Even the *Communist Manifesto* did state that the 'costs' which the worker causes the capitalists 'are almost entirely confined to the means of subsistence that he requires for his maintenance and for the propagation of his race'.[14] This obviously means what the bourgeois economists Malthus and Ricardo first expressed and was later called 'the iron law of wages'. Hence the reason why the *Critique of the Gotha Programme* vigorously attacks Lassalle's 'iron law of wages' is the deeper understanding of the whole structure of capitalist society and of the laws of historical development which scientific Marxism derives from its key concept of 'surplus value'. The idea that wages are the value of labour power and not of labour is *not* merely intended (as some people have thought) to enable Marxist economic theory and science to have a clearer and simpler *conceptual structure*. On the contrary this discovery contains the nucleus of the true essence of class contradictions within capitalist society. It provides a systematic explanation of the material reasons why these class contradictions arose and why they have developed and sharpened in spite of a continuing rise in the productive power of social labour. It also explains why this very rise in productivity eventually creates the 'material' possibility and necessity of a complete abolition of class contradictions in a communist society. By contrast, the theory of the 'iron law of wages' is based partly on natural science and partly on the philosophy of Right. It can neither explain the real social origin of class contradictions nor is it able, except on ethical and idealist grounds, to argue for the necessity of a real 'supersession' of this law and with it of the 'curse' it imposes on the working class. (This is

14. *Selected Works*, vol. 1, p. 40.

why Lassalle's dogma, now adopted by the bourgeois economists, is such a danger to the proletariat's struggle for emancipation.) Once this important connection is realized, the full import of the striking comparison made at the end of section III immediately becomes comprehensible. There Marx says that to base the workers' struggle for emancipation on Lassalle's 'iron law of wages' would be like basing a slave rebellion on the *undernourishment* involved in the slave system.

Equally complex and at first sight obscure motives lie behind Marx's furious and relentless attack in section III on the one socio-economic demand the Gotha Programme makes – the demand for 'establishing producers' co-operatives with State aid'. Here, as with the iron law of wages, Marx's fierce attack is not really against the call for producers' co-operatives as such, but only against the particular role that they play in Lassalle's system. In fact, ten years earlier Marx had actually included 'the establishment of producers' associations and other institutions of use to the working class' among the practical demands of the I.W.A. statues, and in his *Inaugural Address* he hailed the co-operative movement, along with the ten-hour day, as 'up to now the greatest victories of the political economy of labour over the political economy of property'. At that time he even emphatically demanded the 'development of co-operative labour on a national scale', aided by 'the means of the State'. Here, too, there would superficially appear to be no real conflict between Marx's position and the demand made by the draft Gotha Programme. In fact, however, this example of Marx's anger is a vivid expression of a deep and substantive difference between his outlook and that of Lassalle. For Marx was only too well aware of the real nature of this scheme (amply demonstrated in any event by the rest of the Programme). The plan for associations of co-operatives conceived in the 1860s along

'Lassallean' lines (whatever Lassalle himself may originally have said when first advancing this demand) relied much more on *State* aid than on the creation of a co-operative *economy* itself.[15] Its real aim was to use aid to the producers' associations to change the 'limited bourgeois state' into a 'socialist state that would fulfil the ethical idea of freedom' – instead of seeking the necessary *material* preconditions for attaining a *socialist society* in the predominance of the political *economy* of the working class over the political economy of property (which may be furthered, among other things, by producers' co-operatives). This was a flagrant violation of a major principle in the I.W.A. Declaration of Principles which stated that 'the economic emancipation of the working class is the principle aim, which every political movement must serve to advance'. Marx in section III of the *Critique* seeks to demolish the key concept of 'co-operatives based on State credit' as a regression into crude ideological and utopian errors. (This idea has recently found its worthy successors in the equally empty notions of many German socialists about 'socialization' or 'seizing real values'.) Marx reaffirms against these illusions the true materialist and revolutionary meaning of the words 'producers' associations on a national scale' by saying: 'That the workers desire to establish the conditions for co-operative production on a social scale, and first of all on a national scale, in their own country, only means that they are working to revolutionize the present conditions of production, and it has

15. See Engels's remark in a footnote to the 1890 Preface to the *Communist Manifesto*, where he says of the Lassalleans: 'Lassalle personally, to us, always acknowledged himself to be a "disciple" of Marx, and as such stood, of course, on the ground of the Manifesto. Matters were quite different with regard to those of his followers who did not go beyond his demand for producers' co-operatives supported by State credits, and who divided the whole working class into supporters of State assistance and supporters of self-assistance.'

nothing in common with the foundation of co-operative societies with State aid'.

9. *The Kernel of the Critique*

In this passage Karl Marx developed the implications of his strictly materialist position with reference only to 'producers' associations with State aid'. But these are not merely of historical importance. On the contrary, his principle can be applied to the latest efforts of the workers' struggle for emancipation – for example, to the 'socializations' of 1918–20 and to the 'acquisition of real values' of 1921–2. The principle Marx establishes can therefore still serve today as a *touchstone* for distinguishing the different positions adopted on these questions. In fact, it will become even more important in the course of future developments, as the major tactical questions of the social revolution, and the even greater practical tasks of the long transitional period between capitalism and communism, gradually approach nearer to reality. This is the most outstanding aspect of the *Critique* today: more than any other writing of Marx and Engels, it gives us a reliable key for solving the great political and social problems which the working class is now called upon to master. This is at once the most difficult and finest period of its historical development. The great transition from the capitalist to the communist socio-economic order is no longer to be accomplished merely in imagination, but in the hard reality of life. Even the *Communist Manifesto*, otherwise the richest source for the Marxist position on all issues beyond purely economic problems, is in this respect somewhat inadequate. There is the well-known list of the ten transitional demands, intended only for the most initial period of the revolution, and a very abstract and philosophically worded definition of the final aim of communism.[16] Apart from this, there is only the repeated statement that in all revolutionary movements communists have emphasized the 'property issue' as the 'fundamental question' (this naturally includes a long period *after* the establishment of the dictatorship of the proletariat). This emphasis on the 'property issue' can be interpreted in two ways. It can be seen either as a *juridicial problem of distribution* which is capable of solution through changes in the *form of the State*, or 'materialistically' as a *social problem of production* which can only be solved by overthrowing the *economic structure* of society. It is precisely by means of a thorough clarification of these two interpretations that Marx, in the *Critique of the Gotha Programme*, sets out the total contradiction between the ideological state socialism of

16. *Selected Works*, vol. 1, p. 54: 'In place of the old bourgeois society, with its classes and class antagonisms, we shall have an association, in which the free development of each is the condition for the free development of all.' This definition of the *communist concept of freedom* does go a long way beyond Kant's categorical imperative, but is still only a simple inversion of the Hegelian concept of freedom, which is most precisely formulated in the following rather complex passage from Hegel: 'First, there comes the empty abstraction of a concept of general freedom for all, distinct from the freedom of each individual. On the other side, arises the same freedom, equally isolated, for the individual. Each posed for itself is an abstraction without reality. But if both are considered as absolutely identical, and posed in terms of this initial and underlying identity, they become something other than the former concepts which have their meaning only through their non-identity' (*Wissenschaftliche Behandlungsarten des Naturrechts*, Lasson edition, p. 367). Hegel links the freedom of each to the freedom of all, as something of equal value. But in doing so he regards the freedom of the individual only in terms of the freedom of the whole, through which it is realized. Marx, by contrast, makes the free development of each the *precondition* for the correlative freedom of all. In the *Communist Manifesto*, he was not yet able to express this abstract and philosophical concept of freedom in terrestrial and material terms.

Lassalle and his own materialist communism. As he never tires of saying, the Lassalleans do not have communist society as their final aim, but only a dreary middle position. It is true that the latter will have overcome private ownership of the means of production and related 'inequalities' and 'injustices' in the distribution of goods. But in every other respect – economically, ethically and spiritually – it will still bear the stamp of the old capitalist society of today. Specifically, bourgeois *Law* and the bourgeois *State* will not have been totally superseded as the forgotten ideas of a barbarous prehistory. Marx himself, of course, was fully conscious of the fact that the establishment of a dictatorship of the proletariat, and the abolition of private capitalist ownership of the means of production, would not in itself suffice to create a mature communist society 'freely' developing to unimagined heights by virtue of its inherent laws. Indeed, he consciously demonstrated this 'materialist insight' in his letter on the Gotha Programme. For 'between capitalist and communist society there lies the period of the revolutionary transformation of one into the other'. The communal socio-economic order created after the establishment of the dictatorship of the proletariat will be 'a communist society not as it has *developed* on its own foundations, but on the contrary as it has *emerged* from capitalist society'. Consequently for a long time thereafter it still remains subject to the natural laws of capitalist society, which are alien and contrary to its novel character and limit and hinder its free development.

This is *unavoidable* for a communist society that has 'emerged from capitalist society after prolonged travail'. From the superior perspective of Marxist communism, the Lassallean socialism derived from philosophies of Right and the State – and in practice the Social Democratic state socialism of today with its Görlitz Programme derived from

Lassalleanism – can thus be judged guilty of criminal folly. The period of *transition* is necessary and inevitable for historical reasons – Lassallean socialism takes it for an *ideal and final state*. The reason for this is obvious – it has itself never surpassed the 'narrow horizon' of bourgeois conceptions of right, ethics and the State. It maunders in an ideological and utopian fashion about the ideal of a 'just distribution' and complete 'social and political equality' in a 'free state'. The primitive idea of freedoms essentially guaranteed by Law and State is annulled precisely by the grandiose final aim of communism, now already visible to us. It will be replaced by future forms of consciousness in the 'new life' of the 'higher phase of communist society'. We, who are still living in the prehistory of human society, can hardly have any realistic picture of what these will be.

Marx and Lenin insist that these high aims cannot be accomplished by pure thought or by some imaginative power impregnating itself in an airy dream world of the spirit. They can only be achieved on the basis of the material development of the forces of production, in the terrestrial and intramundane reality of concrete social life, by means of terrestrial and intramundane actions. For this reason people call them 'materialists' and believe that they have said something against them. The bourgeoisie has good material reasons for so doing, which cannot be taken from them by theoretical and immaterial means either. The situation of workers is a very different one. They suffer from the 'material' conditions of the present as well as the 'ideal' effects of these conditions. They can only be helped 'ideally' and 'materially' by the complete overthrow of these conditions. No one can or will provide this 'material' help for them, except themselves. That is why every worker must in the end become a *materialist*.

The Marxism of the First International [1924]

On 28 September 1864 it was decided at an international meeting of workers in London to found the International Workingmen's Association. On 25 July 1867, Karl Marx wrote the preface to the first edition of the first volume of *Capital.* Within one single period of history, in the 1860s, both aspects of Marxism attained their full realization: the new autonomous science of the working class attained its developed theoretical form in literature at the same time as the new autonomous movement of the proletariat achieved its practical form in history. The 'silent figure' on the platform of St Martin's Hall who 'presented' the German worker Eccarius to the founding conference of the International Workingmen's Association, also presented the 'real forces' of the incipient world proletarian movement with their theoretical expression which he had evolved after enormous intellectual labour.

The epoch-making event that initiated this new stage in the theory and practice of the working class movement was the American Civil War of 1861–5. After the failure of the revolutions of 1848, all the European countries had undergone a period of unparalleled economic prosperity which had sent the forces of reaction into a frenzied spate of counter-revolutionary orgies. The great economic crisis of 1857 had put an end to this, and (as Marx expressed it) had shown that the apparent victories of reaction in this period had been merely a means of 'providing the ideal conditions of 1848 with the material conditions of 1857'. The great London building strike from 21 July 1859 to 6 February 1860, together with the big spring strike of 1861 which came soon afterwards, had pulled even the least class-conscious unions into the struggle of the 'political economy of the working class' against the 'political economy of the bourgeoisie'. At the same time the employers threatened to bring in cheap continental labour during these struggles and there were in fact already traces in some English industries of increased competition from German workers. This was a *practical* lesson to English workers of the need to have a unified international trade union movement. The European working class was also strongly influenced by the domestic and foreign policies of Bonapartist social imperialism in France, by the liberation movement in Italy and by the abolition of serfdom in Russia in 1861. But it was the great world-historical event of a four-year Civil War between the Northern American states and the slave-owning states of the South which was able to produce the great upsurge in proletarian class consciousness out of which there emerged the European proletariat's first international class organization. It was the Civil War which combined the enormous *political* importance of 'a noble struggle for the liberation of an enslaved race' with a deep *economic* effect on the working and living conditions of the English and French working classes. It is only superficially that the Polish rising of 1863 can be seen as the occasion for the founding of the International in 1864. The European proletariat were far more influenced by the practical economic fact of the American

Civil War, as a result of which English imports of cotton fell from 1140.6 million lbs in 1860 to 309.3 million lbs in 1862. This meant that by October 1862, 60.3 per cent of the spindles and 58 per cent of the looms in the English textile centres were idle, and the English and French textile workers were undergoing mass unemployment and illness from hunger and misery. During this period the English working class, under the heavy pressure of these economic developments, also waged an energetic and heroic resistance against the English government's inclination to intervene in the Civil War on the side of the slave-owning states. These practical contradictions within their own situation and actions taught them the fundamentals of the 'political economy of the working class' which found its organizational and theoretical expression in the founding of the International and in Marx's *Capital*. Marx, in the introduction to the first volume of *Capital*, pointed out the decisive importance of the American Civil War in unshackling a really international revolutionary proletarian movement that would sweep the whole of Europe along with it. 'Let us not deceive ourselves about this' he warns those readers of his work on the European continent who might be inclined to see in *Capital* only the history and theory of capitalist relations of production in one particular country: 'As in the eighteenth century, the American War of Independence sounded the tocsin for the European middle class, so in the nineteenth century, the American Civil War has sounded it for the European working class. In England the progress of social disintegration is palpable. When it has reached a certain point, it must have an effect on the continent.'

The American Civil War of 1861-5 as the 'tocsin' for the European working class! In this expression we can see the revived *revolutionary* enthusiasm of the 1860s. At last, after fifteen years of demoralization and lack of participation by the masses, the revival of the working class was visible all at once in England, France, Germany and Italy. This was already clear from the *Inaugural Address* of 1864, which Marx wrote as the Programme of the new international class organization and which was unanimously adopted with great enthusiasm by the General Committee of the International. It culminates in the passage stating that the *seizure of political power* is the major task which the working class now faces and is the aim of the newly founded international class organization of the European proletariat. This thesis is concretely developed in the demand that the working class in the different countries must also prove its fraternal cooperation by preventing *foreign policy* from 'playing on national prejudices and squandering the peoples' goods and blood in predatory wars', as did Palmerston's policy towards the American Civil War and the Polish Rising, and the policies of Bonapartist France and of Czarist Russia. For this purpose the working class should 'master the mysteries of international politics, watch the diplomatic actions of their governments and counter them, if necessary, by all the means at their disposal.'

It remained for the 'Marxists' of the Second International, for Messrs Kautsky, Hilferding and Co., to falsify these explicit formulations of the revolutionary practice and theory of *the Marxism of the First International*, and to argue that Karl Marx, the revolutionary of 1848, had matured to manhood in the subsequent fifty years, and had been 'converted' to a political 'theory of relativity' based on reforms 'within the capitalist state'. On this basis they contrasted the 'perfected and developed' Marxism of the 1860s which was 'also applicable to non-revolutionary periods' to the 'primitive Marxism of their early works, which Marx and Engels produced in the period from their twenties to the revolution of

1848 and its aftermath in 1849–50' (Kautsky). Hilferding adds the discovery that the present prime minister of England, MacDonald, has 'been carrying out' the foreign policy demanded by the *Inaugural Address* for the international working class in his 'honourable peace policy' aimed at 'uniting the major nations'.

These social democratic agents of capitalism's war and post-war policies have disgracefully abandoned the true theory and practice of Karl Marx and of the First International. Confronted with this, the Third International has before it the task laid down by Lenin of *fulfilling Marx's legacy and translating it into life.* It has undertaken this historical task in a situation which, after the Russian Revolution, reproduces all the political and economic effects that an event like the American Civil War of 1861–5 had on the European working class. These are now being felt by the exploited classes and oppressed people of Europe, America, Asia and the whole world on a far broader scale and with unparalleled intensity. The tocsin of world revolution is sounding from Soviet Russia.

Printed in the United States
By Bookmasters